# THE BAPTISTS OF NORTH EAST ENGLAND

## 1650 - 2000

David F Neil

2006

© David F. Neil


First published in 2006 by the author at 54 Bradley
Avenue, Houghton-le-Spring, Tyne and Wear, DH5 8JY




Printed and bound by
Lintons Printers,
Crook, Co. Durham
Tel. 01388 762197




ISBN: 0-9552715-0-9
978-0-9552715-0-2

# Contents

# Foreword

I consider myself an honorary northerner. Although I was born in Surrey and reared in Hampshire, my father's home city is Liverpool and my mother was born in Consett in County Durham. Most of my summer holidays were spent in the North East visiting my grandmother Mary Willis and the extended family of aunts, uncles and cousins.

My grandparents emigrated to Consett from Ireland at the end of the nineteenth century and my grandfather and uncles were employed by the world famous Consett Iron Company. As a boy I can recall visiting the Iron Company and being overwhelmed by the sounds and smells of this giant industrial complex. My family history has given me a deep appreciation of the unique culture of the North East as well as the faithful Gospel witness of Baptists through the past centuries.

This book is overdue. It is the first comprehensive story in one volume of the Baptists of North East England since 1846 when David Douglas published his 'History of the Baptist Churches in the North of England'. David Neil is well qualified to record this history having served in two pastorates, Whitley Bay and Crook, as well as serving as Association Minister and Secretary of the Northern Baptist Association, and editor of 'The Northerner', the NBA magazine.

He has compiled a wealth of information that is both fascinating and instructive. From small beginnings the story is traced over 350 years, seeing how God used gifted leaders and godly men and women whose desire was to be part of a biblically based and mission focussed movement where Christ was honoured.

The early years were not easy, yet we see in these Baptist pioneers an outstanding consistency of faithful witness. The unfolding story is not one of uninterrupted success and growth. There were periods of spiritual and numerical decline reflecting the seismic changes in the social and economic changes of the North East, yet in each generation there were those who persevered believing that the Lord had plans to prosper them and provide them with a hope and future.

There are sufficient signs in the opening years of the third millennium that Christian witness in the coming decades is going to be one of the most challenging periods for the Church. A strong investment in the discipline of church history enables us to see God's glorious plan of salvation being worked out 'come wind - come weather'. I trust that a careful reading of this history will inspire the present generation of Baptists of the North East to bring their own faithful witness to the transforming power of Jesus Christ.

**David Coffey**
*General Secretary, Baptist Union of Great Britain, 1991-2006*
*President, Baptist World Alliance, 2005-2010*

# Introduction

The main purpose of this book is to provide a factual account of the origins and ongoing life of the Northern Baptist Association and of the Baptist churches which were members of that Association. To tell the full story of eighty churches covering a period of 350 years would require many volumes, but it is hoped that the limited information contained in this one volume will provide a general overall picture of how things developed.

The contents of this book are largely based on four primary sources: (a) the Northern Baptist Association minutes from 1695 onwards, (b) the Association's annual reports, (c) David Douglas' book, 'History of the Baptist Churches in the North of England', published in 1846 (d) the histories of individual churches produced from time to time by the churches themselves. The first three of these sources are in the Association archives held by the Tyne and Wear Archives Service in Newcastle. I had recourse to other secondary sources, but these were consulted mainly to verify or elucidate information on a specific issue. Unfortunately over twenty Association annual reports are missing from the archives, and I was unable to obtain any written history from quite a number of the churches, so this may explain the absence of some information which some readers feel merited inclusion. I have been able to work only with the information available to me.

The initial encouragement to write this book came from David Lennox, the Association Secretary, and I have valued his continuing interest and help. I gave my original manuscript to six friends – John Claydon, John Lauderdale, John Nicholson, Arthur Pearson, Abel Rees and Paul Revill – and their comments and observations have made this a much better book than it otherwise would have been. I thank them for their willingness to help.

No written history is totally objective, and I make no claims for that. However, I have done my utmost to be faithful to the recorded facts. In several places I have attempted an interpretation or drawn a conclusion where information was incomplete, and I leave the reader to judge their relative merits.

In his book 'The Life of Reason' George Santayana, the Spanish philosopher, wrote, "Those who cannot remember the past are condemned to repeat it". Since we can and should learn from our history, I have written a final chapter offering a personal opinion and suggesting lessons that we could learn today from those of former generations whose great desire was to create a church that was true to the teaching of Scripture.

Three final words of additional thanks must be given. I am most grateful to David Coffey for his willingness to write the Foreword. Not only have many in the North East appreciated his interest in and care for the churches of the region, but they also hold him in high regard for the distinguished contribution he has made to Baptist church life both nationally and internationally. I am also grateful to Sir Peter and Lady Margaret Vardy whose generosity through The Vardy Foundation has made possible the production of this book in its present form. But above all my thanks must go to my wife, Ruby, my true helpmeet and companion on life's way for over fifty years, who has not only encouraged me in this project, but has typed – and re-typed – the manuscript.

David F Neil
March 2006

Chapter 1.

# The Protestant Reformation

## The Reformation on the Continent

If we are to have a better understanding of the emergence of Baptist churches in England in the seventeenth century, we need to go back to the Protestant Reformation of the sixteenth century. The two main leaders of the Reformation movement were Martin Luther in Germany and John Calvin in Geneva. Their stand against the Roman Catholic Church resulted in the formation of the Lutheran and Reformed Churches on the continent of Europe.

A third reformer at that time was Ulrich Zwingli, who in 1518 was appointed people's priest in the important parish church of Zurich in Switzerland. Many regard him as the reformer who was the forerunner of the Baptist tradition. He undertook an extensive programme of Biblical preaching which led to a radical programme of reform which was accepted by the Zurich city leaders. Among it features were the acceptance of the Bible as the sole rule of faith and a recognition that the church is made up of converted people. In rejecting the eucharistic sacrifice of the mass, he did not merely replace it with a memorial feast, but saw the bread and wine as a spiritual sign of the presence of the ascended Christ in his body the congregation gathered around the table. He administered baptism on confession of faith, but opposed the rebaptism as believers of those baptised as infants. This latter practice was adopted by most of the radical reformers of the time, hence them being named Anabaptists by their opponents.

From 1525 onwards Zwingli sought, with the backing of the Zurich city council, to suppress Anabaptism because of some of its excesses, but despite this the movement spread to various parts of Europe. Since the aim of the Anabaptists was the establishment of autonomous congregations and not a state church, its members were persecuted by both the Roman Church and other reformation movements. This hostility, compounded with later internal divisions and excesses, weakened and split the movement, but under Menno Simons it underwent further development by freeing itself from some of its earlier excesses. Rufus Jones in his book, 'Studies in Mystical Religion', described the Anabaptist movement as "the spiritual soil out of which all nonconformist sects have sprung". Although a direct 'line of descent' cannot be traced from the Anabaptists to the formation of the first Baptist churches in England, nonetheless the movement's radical spirit which was based on the New Testament teaching came to characterise the early congregations of English Baptists.

## The Reformation in England

When Henry VIII broke with the Pope in 1534 and established the Church of England, his aim was not a radical or spiritual reformation of the Church, such as was occurring on the continent. He was happy for most Roman Catholic practices to continue, but the fundamental change was that he (and not the Pope) was now the head of the national church. Some within the church, however, saw this break with Rome as the opportunity to work for the church's spiritual renewal. Many of these people had been influenced by the continental reformation movement but they were opposed by the king, and some had to flee to the continent from the persecution that the king directed towards them.

When Edward VI succeeded to the throne on Henry's death in 1547 at the age of ten, steps were taken to bring about a genuine reformation of the church. This process of change was at an early stage when Edward died in 1553, and Mary I succeeded him on the throne. Mary - a staunch Catholic – returned the church to papal allegiance, and her cruelty towards the reformers earned her the title of 'Bloody Mary'. These reformers who were either imprisoned or sentenced to death were forced once again into exile on the continent.

Mary reigned for only five years, and when Elizabeth I came to the throne in 1558 she immediately re-established the church as Protestant. However, she had no great liking for Calvinistic Protestantism, and what came to be called the 'Elizabethan Settlement of Religion' (whose main features still largely operate today in the Anglican Church) fell short of the changes sought by the reformers. Those who desired a much more thorough reformation became known as Puritans, so called because of their desire to purify the church of error and malpractice.

The Puritan Party became a significant force, being well represented in Parliament, as well as having members among the bishops, clergy and laity. Initially, the Puritans had no thought of becoming a breakaway movement. Their aim was to work within the church for its renewal. But as the sixteenth century progressed and the Elizabethan Settlement became more firmly established, some Puritans felt that the only way forward was to withdraw from the Anglican Church and establish separatist congregations whose life and doctrine were fully based on what they firmly believed to be New Testament principles. When these first 'separatists' formed themselves into 'gathered churches', many of the other Puritans denounced their action, believing that the true path of reform lay not in separating but in remaining loyal to the established church and working from within for its reformation.

Though some separatist churches may have been formed earlier than 1580, the first record of one being established (which was based on Congregational principles) is that of Norwich in that year, its main leaders being Robert Browne and Robert Harrison. Its members soon faced persecution, some of their leaders being hanged and others having to flee the country. Other similar churches were established in subsequent years, but Elizabeth and the Anglican church authorities were not prepared to tolerate any kind of nonconformity, and efforts were constantly made to suppress these gathered churches. This policy of suppression was followed not only during the reign of Elizabeth but was continued for forty years after her death during the reign of James I and Charles I.

## The First English Baptist Churches

In the early years of the seventeenth century some separatists came to the conviction that the New Testament taught that baptism should be administered only to believers, and it is among these people that we find the origins of Baptist churches in England. Two strands of Baptist life emerged in these early days – the General Baptists (Arminian in theology) and the Particular Baptists (Calvinistic in theology) – and these two groups maintained their separate identities for over 250 years.

John Smyth was ordained into the Anglican priesthood in 1594 and in 1600 was appointed Lecturer to the City of Lincoln. Six years later he identified with a separatist congregation in Gainsborough who appointed him as its pastor, but due to persecution the congregation emigrated to Amsterdam. Smyth's aim was to create a church based on New Testament teaching and one outcome of his study of Scripture was his rejection of infant baptism and the adoption of believers' baptism. The congregation identified with this view, and on being baptised as believers in 1609 they formed themselves into the first English Baptist church.

Thomas Helwys was one of the leaders in this church, and differences arose between him and Smyth with the result that the congregation divided into two groups, one being led by Smyth and the other by Helwys. Smyth adopted Arminian views, and although he died in Amsterdam in 1612 he could be regarded as the founder of the English General Baptists. Helwys and his group returned to England that year, and established the first Baptist church on English soil in Spitalfields in London. His church adopted the Arminian views that had been embraced by Smyth, and they became known as the General Baptists. By 1626 another four General Baptist churches had been established in the country.

At this time Puritans, Congregational separatists and most Anglicans were Calvinistic in their theology. At one of the London Congregational churches discussion took place about baptism, and some members who came to the view that baptism was for believers only were dismissed, albeit in a friendly way, and formed themselves into a church that practised believers' baptism. Although records of this group are scant, it seems that this group which was formed in the 1630s became the first Particular Baptist church. Soon other similar Baptist churches were established, seven of which united in 1644 to publish a Confession of Faith.

These early Baptist churches had a struggle to exist. Not only were they continually facing opposition from the authorities, they were also giving much thought and effort in defining the characteristics of a true church based on New Testament principles, and on some issues it was difficult to reach a common mind. Although records of these early days are not plentiful, we do know, as stated above, that in 1626 there were at least five General Baptist Churches and in 1644 seven Particular Baptist Churches.

# Chapter 2.

# Toleration and Persecution

King Charles I, who succeeded to the throne in 1625, had difficult relations with successive Parliaments over financial, religious and political issues, resulting in him ceasing to call Parliaments after 1629. He exercised personal rule for eleven years, but was forced to recall Parliament in 1640 and make concessions to redress grievances that had built up against him. Two years later he determined to seize back power on his own terms, and by the end of 1643 Parliament and king were deadlocked in a battle to control England.

The years that followed were times of conflict and unrest throughout the country. In 1649 Parliament placed King Charles under house arrest and shortly afterwards had him executed. Oliver Cromwell became the most powerful man in England, and during his time as 'Lord Protector of England' a measure of religious freedom was granted. It was around this time that many new gathered churches were established.

Cromwell's death in 1658 and weak leadership in Parliament caused many to seek after the restoration of the monarchy, and in 1660 Charles II was crowned king. Shortly after this, Anglicanism became the state religion, and municipal officeholders could retain their positions only if they took an oath of allegiance and loyalty to the King and the Church of England.

In July 1662 Charles and Parliament (which was now strongly Royalist) obliterated most of the legislation of the previous twenty years, and the following month by the Act of Uniformity they set the doctrinal and liturgical character of the now established Anglican Church. This act required all clergy by law to swear allegiance to the new state and church, and to use the revised Book of Common Prayer. Around 2000 clergy refused to conform and were dismissed from their parishes (it was this action that caused them to be labelled as 'nonconformists'). Among these clergy were thirty Baptists, none of whom, however, were in the north of England. A view widely held at this time was that the country should have only one church and that to dissent from this was an expression of disloyalty and revolution.

A further repressive act in May 1664 – the Conventicle Act – banned religious gatherings (apart from those in the parish church) of more than five people, its aim being to stop nonconforming clergy from forming their own congregations. Anyone found attending such a 'conventicle' was liable to a fine or imprisonment. A fourth Act in October 1665 – the Five Mile Act – banned nonconforming ministers from living within five miles of any town in which they had previously served unless they swore loyalty to King, state and church.

It should be noted that Parliament passed all these restrictive acts (known as the Clarendon Code) despite all the promises of religious freedom made at the time of the restoration of the monarchy. The enforcement of these laws, however, varied from place to place depending on the local officials. To counteract this, one further repressive act  - the Second Conventicle Act – was passed in April 1670 which laid down that local justices should be fined if they failed to prosecute the nonconformists.

In February 1685 Charles II died and his brother, James II, who had converted to Roman Catholicism, succeeded to the throne. James said he would 'maintain the government of church and state as established by law', but many Anglicans were suspicious. In April 1687 Parliament passed the 'Declaration of Indulgence', granting freedom of worship to nonconformists and suspending previous legislative tests. Many felt that this declaration was made primarily for the benefit of Catholic and not Protestant nonconformists, because within six months over 300 Catholic justices had been appointed.

In May 1688 the Anglican Church opposed the king's attempt to establish the Roman Catholic Church on the same footing as the Anglican Church (Rome had appointed four bishops to serve in England, and James had packed many important councils and bodies with Catholics). The main issue now in the country was the struggle against James in order to keep England a Protestant country.

In response to an invitation William of Orange invaded England in November 1688. Many welcomed him and defected to him, since James' policies had united the Protestants against him. In the following month James fled to France without offering any resistance. William and Mary were crowned King and Queen of England. They were also proclaimed King and Queen of Scotland on the basis of the 'Claim of Rights', an act which stated that the succession to the throne be limited to Protestants. Both the new King and Queen pledged to maintain the 'Protestant Reformed religion as established by law'.

In December 1689 the accession of William and Mary was described as both 'the glorious revolution' and 'the bloodless revolution'. William had no desire for revenge. A 'Bill of Rights' was passed by Parliament. This was in effect a social contract between King and Parliament, two of its main features being Parliament established as the supreme law-making body, and the barring of Catholics from succeeding to the throne.

Also that year the Act of Toleration was passed, thus marking the time when active opposition against nonconformists ceased. Although they still lived under many restrictions, Baptists and other non-conformists now had a legal base to protect their churches. They were able to structure themselves in a way they deemed right without fear of being persecuted and penalised by the state.

# Chapter 3.

# The Early Years 1650-1689

## Baptists in Newcastle

The first Baptist Church in North-East England was formed in Newcastle in 1650, largely through the efforts and leadership of officers in the New Model Army. To strengthen his control over the country, Cromwell stationed his troops in strategic locations throughout the land. Newcastle, then a key town with a population of 13,000 people, had a major army garrison. In 1647 Col. Robert Lilburne was appointed Governor of Newcastle and Lt. Col. Paul Hobson, Deputy Governor. Both these men had Baptist sympathies, as did another officer, Captain Thomas Gower. Hobson and Gower, prior to their posting to Newcastle, lived in London, and both are on record as signatories to the 1644 Baptist Confession of Faith as leaders of a London Baptist congregation. Hobson was probably one of the founders of Crutch Friars Baptist Church in London. In 1650 Col. Mason, also a Baptist, succeeded Lilburne as Governor of Newcastle.

These and other soldiers were among the original members of the Baptist church in Newcastle, Thomas Gower being the first known leader, with Hobson being appointed as an elder. Gower must have settled in the North East, since he served as minister of the church until at least 1669.

The church's first place of meeting was St Thomas' Chapel, Bridge End, located where the swing bridge is today near the Guildhall. A year later (1651) the church moved from there and began meeting in the home of Captain John Turner, another Baptist army officer. Around this time eight companies of the regiment stationed at Newcastle were moved to Carlisle and this resulted in the church losing several of its original members.

Early references to the Baptist church in Newcastle are very few as there are no church records so it is very difficult to build a complete picture of the church in its earliest years. There are references to Baptists meeting in South Shields and Sunderland in the latter part of the seventeenth century, and since records show that Gower lived in Cleadon (midway between these two towns), it is reasonable to assume that the Newcastle church had branch congregations in these two places.

Gower was succeeded as minister by Mr Turner, who was a delegate to the Baptist General Assembly in London in 1689. He was succeeded by Richard Pitts, who pastored the church from 1689 to 1698.

## Baptists in Hexham

In 1650 Parliament established a 'Commission for the Propagation of the Gospel in the Four Northern Counties'. These were Northumberland, Durham, Cumberland and Westmorland. It would seem that this commission was partly a response to a petition sent by the people of Muggleswick (in Derwentside) bemoaning the absence of any spiritual leadership in the churches. They complained that their minister was "one of the most debauched among the sons of men" and that he locked the door of the church to prevent them worshipping on the Sabbath.

A lectureship had been established in Hexham Abbey in 1628 by the Mercers' Company of London. Thomas Tillam decided to apply for this position to the Commission, and he took up his duties as lecturer at Hexham Abbey in December 1651. Tillam's name can still be seen today in the list of Encumbents and Lecturers above the West Door in Hexham Abbey. Tillam was a member of the Coleman Street Baptist Church in London, and that church, along with six other London Baptist churches, appointed him as their 'messenger' (we would regard such a person today as an 'apostle' or an 'evangelist').

On 21 July 1652 Tillam baptised sixteen people who formed themselves into a Baptist church with Tillam as their leader. It is possible that this group originally met in the Chapter House of the Abbey. Some of the founder members were people of importance and influence in the area, among whom were Richard Orde, a landowner, and Stephen Anderton, the Bailiff of Hexham. By the end of the year their number had increased had increased to thirty-six.

On 4 December the church wrote a letter to the Coleman Street Church in London thanking them for sending Thomas Tillam among them. In their reply the church expressed gratitude for the news and affirmed that they owned the Hexham congregation to be a visible constituted church of God to whom they were happy to give the right hand of fellowship.

The church elected John Thirwell as deacon and ordained Edward Hickhorngill as a messenger of the church, setting him aside to work with

9

the newly formed Baptist congregations in Scotland. Although the church continued to grow, in 1653 George Fox, the founder of the Quakers, undertook a preaching tour in the Hexham area, and some of the Baptist church members went over to Quaker congregations.

In March 1653 the church again wrote to the Coleman Street Church in London, this time asking them to consent to Thomas Tillam becoming their pastor. At that time he was the 'messenger' of the London church, and the Hexham church felt it appropriate to have that church's approval before appointing him as pastor. The London church said that they were happy to approve if the church felt he met the Scriptural qualifications for a pastor laid down in Paul's letters to Timothy and Titus.

In their letter, however, they raised an issue which was to cause much distress over the next three years. Apparently Thomas Gower of the Newcastle church had written to the Coleman Street church bringing charges against Tillam. This was to be the beginning of a growing tension between the Newcastle and Hexham churches which eventually resulted in Tillam leaving Hexham in 1656.

Despite this problem the Hexham church continued to grow and spread its influence to Derwent Valley. Among the many who were baptised and added to the church in 1653 were John Ward, who was then 22 years of age, and Henry and Mary Angus. John Ward was to play a major leadership role in the life of the church for over sixty years, and Henry and Mary Angus were the ancestors of the many members of the Angus family who in later years were to make a significant contribution to Baptist life both regionally and nationally.

Thomas Tillam was a charismatic figure and did not confine his labours to Hexham. Being an evangelist he travelled to other parts of the country to engage in evangelistic ventures, and seemed keen to engage in open debate with clergymen about the nature of baptism. In May 1653 he was invited to Stokesley in North Yorkshire. The records of the Hexham church state that Mr Richard Kaye was pastor of a church in Stokesley, and that he and nineteen of his members had invited Tillam to come and baptise them. Tillam went and was accompanied by seven of the Hexham church members, and on 3 July 1653 he baptised Kaye and his nineteen friends, thus establishing the Stokesley Baptist Church.

The happenings at Stokesley encouraged the Hexham church to renewed outreach, and as a result eight residents of Muggleswick came to faith and were baptised, their baptism in the River Derwent causing considerable local attention and interest. An unusual feature was that three paedo-baptist clergymen were present planning to use this opportunity to dispute with Tillam about baptism. It would seem that Tillam won the day because six persons who witnessed this public disputation asked to be baptised on the spot. During 1653 thirty eight persons had been baptised and added to the church.

Since Baptist principles were being diffused throughout the country, not least through many of Cromwell's soldiers who were of Baptist persuasion, an attempt was made to develop fellowship among the Baptist churches that had been established. Three London Baptist churches, including the Coleman Street church, wrote to the church at Hexham expressing a desire for greater communication between them, and similar moves were seen in other parts of the country. The Hexham church received a letter signed by the leaders of eight Baptist churches in Herefordshire, Monmouthshire, Gloucester, Worcestershire and London which displayed a real interest in each other's affairs.

Towards the end of 1653 Thomas Gower, leader of the Newcastle church, adopted a vindictive attitude, almost appearing as personal enmity, towards Thomas Tillam. In a letter to the Hexham church he listed twelve accusations against Tillam, but the church responded by affirming Tillam's integrity. A second letter came from the Newcastle church accusing Tillam of acting dishonourably, to which the Hexham church responded once again speaking in Tillam's defence. One sentence in their letter is worthy of mention – "we desire you would seriously lay to heart how mightily our Lord Jesus suffers through our divisions".

The Newcastle church persisted in their accusations, complaining that the Hexham church 'had come out of Babylon only by halves', implying that the church was not prepared to base its practice fully on New Testament principles. Baptists at this time were sorting out their doctrine of the church. Their great desire was to have a gospel church based on New Testament teaching, so when differences of New Testament interpretation arose, those differences often took on a prominence and even caused division that we today, looking back, find strange.

Thomas Gower maintained that in a true gospel church, authorisation for ministry could come only from the baptised congregation and should be totally separated from any involvement with state structures. The fact that Tillam's appointment at Hexham was by the state, that he fellowshipped

11

with Presbyterian and Independent ministers, and that he supported the open membership position of the newly-formed Baptist church at Stokesley, all meant in Gower's view that Tillam was still 'half living in Babylon'. We do not know all that transpired between the churches at Newcastle and Hexham, but Gower took the matter further by contacting the Coleman Street Church in London about the issue. The result was that the Coleman Street church withdrew its support of Tillam as its messenger, and a further consequence was that several of the Hexham members withdrew from membership of the church. This suggests there may have been fault on the part of Tillam, but the rancour marked by the dispute caused great distress.

The content of the twelve accusations have not been left on record, but it would appear that among them were differing views about the nature and upkeep of the ministry, the practice of laying on of hands (after baptism, blessing of children, ordination of deacons, etc.), and Tillam's associating with paedo-baptist ministers. In addition, there is some indication that Gower was aggrieved at Tillam starting a new church in Hexham rather than establishing it as an extension of the Newcastle church. Tillam became unhappy about the whole situation and made the decision, not without pain, to leave Hexham in 1656.

From his writings it is evident that Tillam was a man of piety, of great energy and possessing a loving, affectionate spirit. There may have been indiscretions and failures that caused Thomas Gower to be so stinging in his reproofs and accusations against him, but it cannot be denied that Tillam's time at Hexham was greatly blessed of God.

**Extensions from the Hexham Church**

On Tillam's departure the church at Hexham had over eighty members, and they divided into two sections, each section being led by an elder. It would seem that a contributory factor in this division was the controversy between Gower and Tillam, and for several months there was no communication between the two sections. Happily, however, reconciliation was reached within a year, but despite this they agreed that they would continue to meet as two separate churches. Following Tillam's departure the Hexham congregation was led by Richard Ode, and began to meet in Juniper Dye House, three miles south of the town. The Derwentside congregation was led by John Ward, who lived in Muggleswick.

As already mentioned in the previous chapter, the restoration of the monarchy in 1660 was to have serious consequences on civil and religious liberties, bringing to an end a period of twenty years during which the independent churches throughout the country saw considerable growth. For the next twenty eight years, initially under the leadership of the Earl of Clarendon, persecution and suffering against nonconformists reached a level that has rarely been seen in any other period, though the severity of this action was experienced more in the south than in the north of the country, since of the 297 Baptist churches known to exist in 1660 only nine of these were located in the northern counties.

In 1662 Mr John Elrington of Blanchland reported to the magistrates that the Anabaptist members of the Derwentside and Newcastle churches had held secret meetings at Muggleswick to plot the overthrow of Parliament and the murder of all bishops and ministers of the established church. News of this so-called plot caused alarm in Durham, and Bishop Cosin (an ardent royalist) imprisoned some of the church leaders and made plans to counteract this supposed uprising. He instigated a search for Thomas Gower and Paul Hobson of the Newcastle church, describing them as "two of the most dangerous fellows in the north". All those imprisoned were eventually released since no corroborative evidence could be found to substantiate Elrington's accusations, but for some time afterwards the Derwentside and Newcastle churches were marked and carefully watched by the authorities. Robert Surtees in his History of Durham describes Elrington as an 'infamous scoundrel', and it is now generally accepted that the 'Muggleswick conspiracy' had no basis in fact, but was a plot hatched up in Elrington's mind to discredit the dissenters.

Mr Henry Blacket, who lived at Bitchburn Farm near Bishop Auckland, identified with the Baptist congregation at Derwentside, and around 1663 he was ordained co-pastor of the church with John Ward, and served in that position till his death in 1705. Shortly after this a congregation began meeting at Blacket's farm in Bitchburn, and another congregation was established at Hindley Farm near Broomley. Thus the Derwentside church met in three locations – Eadsbridge (near Muggleswick), Bitchburn and Broomley.

In the early 1670s the Hexham church had reached a very low condition while in contrast the Derwentside church flourished. This may have been partly the result of the stringent local application of the Conventicle Act. This Act made church meetings illegal, but because the Derwentside church met by using remote country farmhouses they were able to continue largely unmolested in a way that was impossible in a town like Hexham.

In 1674 the Derwentside and Newcastle churches actively worked for the renewal of the Hexham church and their efforts were rewarded. As a result of the help received the members of the Hexham church held a meeting on 27 December of that year to rededicate themselves to the Lord and from then on the church began to see growth.

John Ward, co-pastor of the Derwentside church, was described as a 'skillful mineralogist'. He was probably an agent in the local lead mines and his work involved him travelling to the mines in the Furness area of North Lancashire every eight weeks. It would seem that he engaged in evangelism on these business visits, because a Baptist church was formed at Torver in 1678, and a church record states that it was through the efforts of John Ward and Robert Blenkinsop, messengers and elders of the church at Derwentside, that the church came into being.

Although we think of there being only three Baptist churches in the North East in the seventeenth century, these being at Hexham, Derwentside and Newcastle, there is clear evidence that Baptists were present in other areas. The Bishop of Durham's Visitation Books and Episcopal returns, which among other information gave details of indictments against dissenters, refer to Anabaptists, as they were then called by the authorities, who lived in South Shields, Sunderland, Brancepeth, Witton, Hamsterley and Medomsley.

There are no written documents of any of the northern churches from 1682 to 1696, but it can rightly be assumed that the Revolution of 1688 came as a great relief to nonconformist churches, since it brought to an end a generation of persecution in which many of their members were either fined, imprisoned, executed or deported. Following the new atmosphere of freedom brought about by the 1689 Toleration Act, united meetings of dissenting churches, began to be held in various parts of the country.

The Particular (or Calvinistic) Baptists held a national General Assembly of their churches from the third to the twelfth of September 1689, and among those attending were Richard Pitts and John Turner representing the Newcastle church as well as representatives from the Derwentside church. It would seem that one outcome of this gathering was that the churches in different districts were recommended to form themselves into Associations, since the letter calling the General Assembly for the following year lists twelve Associations with a total membership of 103 churches.

One of these twelve was the Northern Baptist Association, formed in 1690 with a membership of six churches. These six founding churches were Pontefract (Yorkshire), Wolverstone (incorporating Tottlebank, Hawkshead-hill and Torver), Durham (incorporating Derwentside, Broomley and Bitchburn), Newcastle (with congregations in South Shields and Sunderland), Egremont and Broughton. This clearly indicates that originally membership of the Association was not confined to the historic counties of Northumberland and Durham, but included churches in Yorkshire, Cumberland and North Lancashire. Although the official record says the Association was made of six churches, there were in fact twelve or thirteen congregations.

We know nothing of the Baptist churches in Pontefract and Egremont. The Broughton church had been founded in 1648 by army officers stationed in the nearby Cockermouth Castle. In 1669 a Baptist church was founded in Tottlebank near Ulverston (then called Wolverstone) and several years later it was the means of another church being formed a few miles further north in Hawkshead Hill. It should be noted, however, that some Baptist churches in Yorkshire, known to have been formed before 1690 are not included in the General Assembly's list of churches, though some years later they are represented at the annual assembly of the Association.

**The Angus Family**

Many members of the Angus family have a honoured place not only in North East Baptist life but in national and international affairs. Since their contribution covers most of the period of this book, perhaps it is appropriate to include something about them here. In 1955 Angus Watson wrote a book for private circulation entitled The Angus Clan (1588 to 1950) and in it he claims that a Baptist fellowship existed in North East England at least thirty years prior to the establishment of the first recorded Baptist church in Newcastle in 1650.

The earliest confirmed record of the Angus family is 1584 when Alexander Angus moved from Scotland and acquired Juniper Dye House, three miles south of Hexham. It would seem that other members of the family also moved since there are records of them living in Raw House, Dotland Park, Ardley, Dilston, Hindley and Panshields, all locations in Hexhamshire a few miles from the town of Hexham.

While in Scotland the Angus family showed sympathy to the views of the Huguenots, a French Protestant and mainly Calvinistic group, and their move to North East England was prompted by the religious persecution that they faced in Scotland. Once settled they began to meet together for fellowship in Alexander Angus' home at Juniper Dye. Henry Angus is on record as having 'professed the religious principles of the Baptists' in 1620. He became known as 'the Patriarch', because many of his descendants were to contribute significantly to Baptist life in the region.

Although this is anticipating the future chapters of this book, it is worth recording briefly at this point some information about the more notable members of the family.

Jonathan Angus of Panshields became a deacon of the Rowley church in 1720, and gave distinguished leadership to the church during the fifty years he held that office. His son, George Angus, was the leading deacon at Rowley when it formally separated from Hamsterley in 1785, and for many years he was the guiding hand in the challenges and difficulties the church faced in its transition to becoming an independent congregation. When he died in 1815 aged 90 years, his passing was widely mourned.

When the farmhouse at Hindley was closed for public worship in 1835 due to the new building being erected at Broomley, it was said that it had been various members of the Angus family who had been mainly responsible for the worship there for over 150 years.

George Fife Angus (1789-1879) was a key person in establishing Sunday School work in Newcastle. He later moved to London and was one of the founders of the National Provincial Bank of England. He became director of a company that traded with Australia and is looked upon as the founder of the state of South Australia. Several streets and buildings in it capital, Adelaide, are named after him.

Joseph Angus (1816-1902) was a member of the Tuthill Stairs in Newcastle, and distinguished himself as a student at the University of Edinburgh. He became secretary of the Baptist Missionary Society, and then for forty-four years served as President of the ministerial training college at Regent's Park in London. He was one of the Biblical scholars responsible for the Revised Version of the Bible which was published in 1881.

Four members of the Angus family served on the committee of the Northern Baptist Association in the early 1900s, and it was their personal and financial support that enabled some newly planted churches to become well established.

The contribution of the Angus family to North East Baptist life merits a book on its own, but perhaps these few facts will convey something of their influence and impact on so many people.

## Baptists Churches formed between 1650 and 1700 and having a link with the Northern Baptist Association

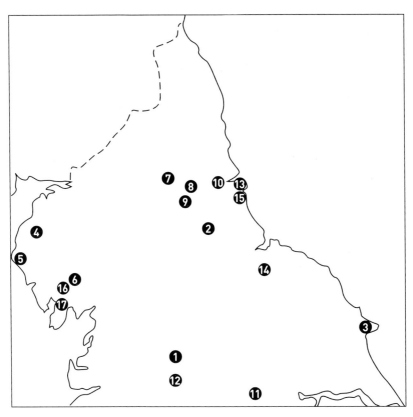

| 1. | Barnoldswick | 7. | Hexham | 13. | South Shields |
| 2. | Bitchburn | 8. | Hindley | 14. | Stokesley |
| 3. | Bridlington | 9. | Muggleswick | 15. | Sunderland |
| 4. | Broughton | 10. | Newcastle | 16. | Torver |
| 5. | Egremont | 11. | Pontefract | 17. | Tottlebank |
| 6. | Hawkshead Hill | 12. | Rossendale | | |

# Chapter 4.

# Development of Association Life: 1690-1732

There are no copies of the minutes of the Association until 1699, but we do know that in 1698 a Baptist Church was established in Bridlington with the pastors of Newcastle, Bitchburn and Derwentside churches being present at its formation, and it immediately became a member church of the Association.

The first minuted meeting of the Association was held in April 1699 at the home of Henry Blacket's son-in-law at Newton Cap, near Bishop Auckland. The records show that messengers (i.e. delegates) came from the churches at Derwentside, Bitchburn, Newcastle, Egremont, Broughton, Rossendale, Barnoldswick, Bridlington, Pontefract and Aughton.

The Association functioned very much like a forum – a meeting together of church representatives to discuss and decide on issues of common concern. These issues were both doctrinal and practical, and were discussed with a view to furthering the welfare of the member churches. The annual assembly was normally a two-day event to which each church was expected to send two messengers. Prayer, preaching and worship took place several times during the two days. After the opening worship there would be the reading of letters from the churches as well as verbal reports by their messengers. The remainder of the two days was taken up by question and answer sessions.

The minutes are largely in the form of questions and answers, and in 1699 sixteen questions were raised. The answers given were the messengers' response to these issues in the light of the teaching of Scripture. Some indication of the seriousness with which they took Scripture (and of their comprehensive knowledge of it) can be adjudged by the fact that the answers include no fewer than sixty-nine references to various Biblical passages. This pattern of question and answer is repeated in subsequent years, again with constant reference to Scripture (for example, the 1701 minutes have 116 Scripture references, many of which are Biblical passages and not simply single verses).

At the 1699 assembly several important issues were discussed, four main ones being how we come to an understanding of what constitutes a true gospel church, the proper exercise of church discipline, the financial support of pastors, and whether elders should be the only ones taking part in Sunday worship or whether all members should be encouraged to participate according to their gifting.

Although space forbids the giving of a comprehensive survey of the issues discussed at the annual assemblies, some of the contents of the 1700 meeting, which was also held at Newton Cap, reveal the wide range of their concern. Twelve questions were raised, four of which addressed the following issues: Should baptised believers frequently sit under the ministry of those who are unsound in any fundamental truth of the gospel? Should a man who is illiterate be given the opportunity to preach if he is so gifted by the Spirit? What can we do more than we are doing now to win sinners to Christ? Is it a Christian duty to pray earnestly for the conversion of the Jews?

As can be seen from the above, their primary concern was that the life of the local church must in every respect reflect the model of church life portrayed in the New Testament. This concern affected worship, membership, ministry and discipline. Since many of these early Baptists thought that the 'perfect' church was attainable, whenever the ideal was not reached they had a responsibility to identify the things causing the failure and deal with them. Thus they were constantly 'exposing' lack of use of God-given gifts, backsliding, lack of faith and love, and so on. This led to constant calls for repentance and prayer to God to forgive past failures. Since they accepted that the rule of Scripture should also regulate every part of the individual Christian's life, discipline of church members was also essential if the church was to achieve the ideal.

One important principle that was accepted by all was that each individual congregation was responsible to Christ as head of the church and must be free to implement Scriptural teaching as they understood it. Although the autonomy of the local church was safeguarded, whenever an issue of importance rose in a church, that church was encouraged to submit that issue to the Association so they could come to a better common understanding about what the Bible had to say about it.

One very interesting feature of their deliberation is that when they could find no clear guidance from Scripture on a particular issue, they clearly stated this and acknowledged the right of each church to determine its own position even though this meant adopting varying standpoints. Differences at this level were never looked upon as barriers to true fellowship.

It is in the context of being churches pleasing to God that we should understand the prominence frequently given to matters of church discipline. The reason for such discipline was not primarily to punish offending members. Rather, they felt discipline was essential if they were to be serious in being a pure gospel church based on New Testament principles. After all, if they were unconcerned about being a pure church on any matter, why should they bother about being a separate church with all its attendant hardships and restrictions, and not just throw in their lot with the local parish church.

From 1701 to 1705 the Association churches held their annual assembly at Bitchburn, the residence of Henry Blacket. The fact that most of those early meetings were held there would suggest that Blacket played an important role in the organisation of Association life. His death in 1705 was a great loss both to the Association and the Bitchburn church. He had been pastor for forty-two years and a tribute paid by his successor, William Carr, portrayed him as a zealous preacher, a wise church governor, and a man of great liberality in both the areas of finance and hospitality.

A matter frequently raised at Association meetings in those early days centred around the ministries of leadership and preaching. The churches recognised the three offices of pastor, elder and deacon, but they used these terms to describe a function rather than a position. Each local church was responsible for deciding its own most appropriate pattern of leadership and the numbers holding the various positions. They also acknowledged the need to recognise these members who were gifted for the preaching ministry. Such members were recognised only after a public test of their suitability had been made. Nobody was allowed to preach until they had been authorised by the local church, but once the church had recognised a man's preaching ability, it was the church's responsibility to provide opportunities for the gift to be exercised. This understanding of ministry threw the emphasis squarely upon the church, emphasising their duty and responsibility to perceive the gifts within its own ranks, especially that of preaching. Members were expected to offer their gifts freely to the church and to improve them, since these were gifts given to them by Christ for the building up of the fellowship. This whole issue was given detailed consideration at the 1706 assembly, the subject being introduced at length by William Carr, the recently appointed pastor of the Bitchburn church.

The theological position of the churches in the Northern Baptist Association was Calvinistic. There is no reason to doubt that they took as their standard the Baptist Confession of Faith agreed at the 1689 national assembly. From 1699 fears were expressed about Arian and Arminian tendencies that were being spread abroad, and although the expression of these views was more prominent in the south than in the north, they were regarded as important enough to merit discussion on several occasions by the Northern Association at its assembly.

In 1717 the Particular Baptists of London organised a fund for the better and more regular provision of Baptist ministers. This scheme was national in its scope, and some grants were received by pastors in northern churches. In 1723 the Association established the practice of taking up an annual collection which was to be disposed of by the assembly delegates 'at their discretion as they judge it may best serve the interest of the churches'.

# Chapter 5.

# Churches and Association 1689-1774

### The Derwent/Bitchburn Church

Following Henry Blacket's death in 1705, meetings of the Bitchburn congregation and the Association Assembly continued to be held in his home at Bitchburn until 1714. That year a new development for the congregation and also for the Northern Baptists occurred – the decision to erect a Baptist meeting house at Hamsterley. This was one of the first dissenting chapels built in the north of England, and it was to be the meeting place for the Association Assembly on eleven occasions between 1715 and 1733. It was said that one reason for the meetings taking place at Hamsterley was ease of access!

In 1717 John Ward died aged 87 years. He had been a member of the Derwentside church for 65 years and pastor for fifty-two years. When Thomas Tillam left Hexham in 1656, John Ward became the person on whose shoulders the care of the Derwentside congregation largely rested. When he died he left his library of 180 books for the benefit of his successors in the ministry, and the list of its contents suggests he was not only a theologian but a classical scholar. He was described as a man of piety, talent, energy and perseverance. Under his leadership the church had grown and had become the most important church in the Association in terms of size and influence.

The deaths of Blacket and Ward removed the two main leaders of the early Baptist cause in the North East. These two leaders had taught a young member of the church, William Carr, and in 1708 he was appointed co-pastor and was to become a worthy leader, serving the church till his death in 1748. It was under his leadership the Hamsterley building was erected, and he also oversaw the erection of a meeting place at Cold Rowley for the Derwentside congregation in 1717.

That year the arrangement was made that Carr would preach on alternate weeks at Hamsterley and Cold Rowley, and this practice continued for many years. In addition to his pastoral and preaching duties, Carr served as moderator (that is the presiding officer) of the Association for six years, and he and the other officers in the church gave leadership and support to other churches in the Association.

Carr was blessed with several lay leaders of quality during his pastorate. Two worthy of mention are Michael Wharton and Jonathan Angus. Wharton was converted in 1710 through the ministry of the Bitchburn congregation, and on his death in 1746 the church thanked God for his Biblical teaching and for his ministry of encouraging, feeding and building up the church of Christ. In 1720 Jonathan Angus was elected a deacon of the Rowley congregation – a position he held for fifty years – and he proved a great helpmeet to Carr, making a significant contribution to the Baptist cause throughout the North East.

At this time the church described itself as 'the Church commonly meeting at Hamsterley and Cold Rowley', but the Hexham congregation meeting at Juniper Dye House and the congregation at Hindley both looked upon themselves as part of that church. Many small Baptist groups also identified with it, looking to it for guidance and help. One such group met at Knaresdale (between Alston and Haltwhistle), this being a congregation which came into existence around 1710 as a result of preachers from the church visiting the area.

A letter from the church at Broughton to the 1741 Assembly recommended one of their members, Isaac Garner, then 24 years of age, to the Association churches, and shortly after that assembly Garner moved to Hamsterley and identified with the congregation there. In 1748 William Carr died after a long and useful ministry in the church, and Isaac Garner was appointed as his successor. Although Garner had an effective ministry in the Hamsterley/Rowley church, including the branch congregations, he exercised a wider ministry and preached periodically at Cotherstone, Newbiggin, Middleton-in-Teesdale, Prudhoe, Horsley and Stamfordham.

In 1750 David Fernie was baptised at Hamsterley by Isaac Garner, and two years later was appointed his assistant and co-pastor. Shortly after this, Fernie began preaching what were described as 'high Calvinistic notions', and this caused a controversy between Garner and Fernie which resulted in the church itself being divided. A crisis point was reached when the two parties mutually withdrew from each other. David Fernie was supported by the Hexham congregation at Juniper Dye House, while Isaac Garner retained oversight of the three congregations at Hamsterley, Rowley and Hindley Farm.

Jonathan Angus, a deacon of the Rowley congregation, wrote a lengthy letter to Isaac Garner expressing sadness at the division, maintaining that the differences did not merit separation since both parties were 'sound in the faith and the fundamental principles of the gospel', and both pastors were proclaiming the same truths which had been the basis of the church's life for many years. Angus does not mention in his letter the specific points on which the two parties differed, nor are they on record elsewhere, but it is probable that the differences were similar to the ones between the 'hyper-Calvinists' and the 'moderate Calvinists' that were seen among the Particular Baptist churches in the south of the country during the eighteenth century.

William Angus of Juniper Dye House, whose home was the meeting place of the Hexham congregation, took the side of Fernie, while his brother Jonathan of the Rowley congregation took the side of Garner. Effectively there were now two separate churches – the Hamsterley/Rowley/Hindley church led by Garner, and the Hexham church under the leadership of Fernie. William Angus invited Fernie to stay with him in his home at Juniper Dye House, and Fernie taking up residence there resulted in an unexpected incident which was to have repercussions on the national Baptist scene.

A young man, Robert Hall, who lived a few miles from Hexham, admitted to being under 'great distress of mind', and he found a measure of relief in identifying with a Presbyterian church. His older brother, Christopher, had previously identified with the Baptists, had become one of their preachers, and had married the daughter of William Angus in whose house the church met. Robert and two of his student friends, James Rutherford and William Peden, felt that the Baptists were 'pernicious heretics', and decided to challenge them about their views. Under the pretext of calling on his in-laws, Robert and his friends visited Juniper Dye House, mainly to meet David Fernie. Fernie welcomed them and for two hours they engaged in vigorous debate. Fernie, who had recently left Presbyterianism to identify with the Baptists, was well versed in the arguments that were used to justify paedo-baptism, and used his knowledge well to counteract what was being said by the three young men.

Following this encounter, Hall began to study the Scriptures and read any book on the subject he could lay his hands on. He returned later to David Fernie, not to engage in further combat but to ask to be baptised by him as a believer in the Lord Jesus Christ. His baptism took place on 5 January 1752, and six months later the church recognised him as a preacher of the gospel.

The significance of this story is that the following year, largely as a result of the recommendation of his brother Christopher, he became pastor of the Arnesby Baptist Church near Leicester, a position he held till his death in 1791. He became a significant Baptist leader, having an important influence on Andrew Fuller, William Carey and other leading Baptists who did so much to further Baptist witness at the time. Andrew Fuller, the first secretary of the Baptist Missionary Society, said of him, "He was eminently skilled for imparting advice; it would be difficult to conceive a human mind more completely purged from the leaven of pride or of envy". Hall wrote a book, 'Help to Zion's Travellers' (1781) which became a classic in Baptist circles, and after reading it, William Carey said, "I do not remember to have read any book with such raptures".

Hall had a son, also called Robert (1764-1831), and he was to become even more distinguished than his father in his leadership among Baptist churches. He ministered in Cambridge, Leicester and Bristol where his great oratorial powers drew large congregations.

Christopher Hall, Robert's older brother, became pastor of the Baptist church at Whitehaven, and then in 1660 moved to Harvey Lane Baptist Church in Leicester, where two of his successors in the pastorate were William Carey and Christopher's nephew, Robert Hall, Junior.

Let us return to the North East of the 1750s. Isaac Garner died in 1758 when only 41 years of age, having pastored the church at Hamsterley for sixteen years. During his ministry seventy four persons were added to the church, and his passing was widely mourned. He was known as a considerable student of Scripture, a good preacher and a holy man. Following his death the Hamsterley congregation was pastorless, and the care of the members and the teaching ministry were undertaken by the deacons.

**The Newcastle Church**

There are very few records of the Newcastle church covering the years following the Restoration, and although the church had a continuing existence, there is no information as to where it met between 1688 and 1720. At the Association Assembly in 1704 concern was expressed about the weak state of the Newcastle church, and this concern was raised again in 1706. In fact, for the first sixty years of the eighteenth century the main records of the church are appeals to other churches for help. Their basic problem seems to have been a lack of quality leadership such as was seen, for example, in the Hamsterley/Rowley church.

In 1720 Mr George West, a wealthy member, purchased a building on Tuthill Stairs for the use of the church, the lower part being the meeting house and the upper part being the dwelling for the minister. The church used this building as its meeting place until 1797. In 1723 the church's donation to the newly established Association Fund was noted as being from the 'the church of Newcastle, Shields and Sunderland', confirming that the church had three congregations.

In 1749 James Kendall, a member of the Tuthill Stairs congregation, wrote to the church at Hamsterley, speaking of the 'poor, reduced and distressed condition of the Newcastle church, now with few members, most of whom are women'. In his letter he asked the Hamsterley church to send two or three of their members to help them.

David Fernie, now living at Juniper Dye House, responded to yet another appeal for help from the Newcastle church at the end of 1752 in which he was asked to sustain the teaching ministry in the church. Fernie took with him two others who had recently been recognised as preachers. These two others were James Rutherford and William Peden, the two young student friends of Robert Hall who had accompanied Hall on his visit to David Fernie to challenge him on the matter of baptism. Both these young men had been baptised by Fernie shortly after Hall's baptism. David Fernie and his two young preachers continued ministering at Newcastle until 1754 when the church called its own minister. That year Peden became minister of the Baptist church in Sunderland (but sadly died within four years) and Rutherford became pastor of a Baptist church in Dublin.

We do not know the reason, but a further appeal was sent by the Newcastle church asking David Fernie to help them once again. In this letter they described themselves as 'young, weak, few, poor and much dispersed'. The last-named description was prompted by the fact that a number of their members did not live in the town, some residing in North Shields and South Shields where they met as separate congregations.

David Fernie once again helped the church by ministering once a month between 1762 and 1769 and this resulted in close links being established between the Hexham and Newcastle congregations. In 1765 he baptised two men, Caleb Elder and Philip Nairn, who were to give excellent service to the Newcastle church in subsequent years. In addition to this help, Fernie continued to exercise a wide ministry, and visits to other churches in Scotland and England were a means of encouragement and blessing.

Perhaps as a result of a visit of David Fernie to London, the Newcastle church in 1769 called John Allen, minister of Petticoat Lane Baptist Church in London, to be their pastor, and although he only remained in Newcastle for two years before moving to America, he baptised several people, one of whom was a young man named Charles Whitfield, who was shortly to become the leading Baptist minister in the North East of England for almost fifty years.

## South Shields and Sunderland

Apart from the mention of the donation of the Newcastle church to the Association Fund in 1723 as coming from 'the church at Newcastle, Shields and Sunderland', there are no Baptist records of any church in South Shields in the eighteenth century. However, in 1734 the curate of St Hild's Church in the town sent a report to the Bishop of Durham in which he says, "in South Shields we have two sorts of dissenters, Presbyterians and Anabaptists, and of both, there is commonly reported to be forty families. We have two licensed meeting houses, one of which is for the Anabaptists". We can only conclude that these Anabaptists made up the South Shields congregation of the Newcastle church. The earliest Baptist record in the town relates to the founding of Westoe Road church in 1818 as an extension of the North Shields church.

Although there are suggestions that some people in Sunderland identified with the Newcastle church in the seventeenth century, and the fact that in 1723 the Newcastle church was described as 'the church in Newcastle, Shields and Sunderland', the earliest firm record of Baptists in that town is 1748 when a meeting house was opened in Ettrick Garth. David Fernie, when he was minister at Juniper Dye House, sent William Peden to minister to the Sunderland church in 1752 and occasionally he ministered to these people himself. This congregation met in a meeting house in Chapel Street, and David Fernie is on record as visiting Baptist churches in the south of England in 1769 to raise funds for the erection of a chapel in Sunderland. We have very few records of this group, but it would seem that a Mr Bowser was minister of the church from 1762 to 1780 and that the church began to meet in new premises in Malins Rigg in 1777. The church ceased to meet sometime during the 1780s, but in 1797 some Sunderland residents who were members of the churches in Newcastle and Hamsterley formed themselves into a new Baptist church in the town and the following year a new building was opened in Sans Street.

## Marton and Stockton

It the mid-eighteenth century Baptists were living in the Stockton area, though they did not constitute themselves into a church. One of these persons was Mr Thomas Angus who had moved from Derwentside. He had a high regard for David Fernie of Juniper Dye House, and Angus asked Fernie if he would come to Teesside and preach. Fernie consented and made his first visit in 1752 and soon his visits to the area became a regular feature. Some residents of Marton, a village six miles south of Stockton (today a suburb of Middlesbrough), responded to this preaching. They formed themselves into a Baptist church in 1754, and shortly afterwards built their own meeting place in the village. In 1766 Fernie was described as pastor of the churches at Marton, Hexham and Newcastle.

David Fernie became known in this area, and was invited to make preaching visits to other towns and villages further into Yorkshire, and as a result churches were established in Bedale, Masham, Dishforth and Boroughbridge.

Around this time the son of David Fernie moved to Stockton to live, and he opened his house for meetings at which his father preached one Sunday each month. A number of people who attended these meetings were members of the Marton church and sometime in the 1770s this group formed themselves into a Baptist church, which later became known as Stockton Tabernacle.

## The Association

In its early days, most meetings of the Northern Baptist Association were held in Weardale (Bitchburn/Hamsterley), but from 1723 the Association Assembly began to be held periodically at Bridlington (mostly alternating with Hamsterley). George Braithwaite, the able minister of the Bridlington church since 1713, gave significant leadership not only to his own church but to the other churches of the Association. It could be argued that around this time Bridlington was the strongest of all the Association churches. The north lost a Christian leader of great ability in 1733 when George Braithwaite accepted the invitation to the pastorate of the Devonshire Square Baptist Church in London.

In 1723 the Association agreed a constitution. This not only regulated its affairs, but clarified the relationship between the Association and the churches. An important point was that the Association should not do anything that violated the autonomy of the local church. The constitution provided for the annual election of a moderator to conduct its meetings and for a clerk to record the proceedings. It is interesting to note that between 1723 and 1733 the only two to serve as moderators were George Braithwaite and William Carr.

As mentioned earlier, a wide range of subjects occupied the minds of those attending the annual assemblies. At the 1725 assembly one question that was considered was, "Whether it would be orderly for church members to marry such as cannot give a demonstration, in some measure, of a work of grace in the hearts of those to whom they are united?" This matter had been discussed at four earlier assemblies, but following the 1725 assembly a lengthy letter was sent to all the churches giving the judgment that Scripture prohibits such a marriage. The letter recommends that churches should not encourage such a practice, since to do so could, in their view, bring God's judgment on the church. The welfare of all the churches and their members became an increasing concern at assembly meetings, and often decisions were made to help these fellowships that were going through periods of difficulty.

David Douglas, commenting on the decisions made at the various assemblies, says, "Those men, though employed in business, were nevertheless mighty in the Scriptures, and far exceed our expectations in the clearness of their views, and the forcible manner in which they express them".

Although annual assemblies continued to be held, there are no records of Association meetings between 1733 and 1740. In fact there are few extant records of both churches and Association. One clue which may explain this is found in the minutes of the 1732 Assembly. They bemoaned the lack of leaders and gifted men within the churches and noted that some gifted members had moved to other parts of the country.

The minutes of the 1740 Assembly speak of a general spiritual decline. Its letter to the churches that year complains of the decrease of both piety and numbers, and also of differences that existed between ministers and members.

From 1739 onwards the national religious life of the country was beginning to be greatly affected by the itinerant preaching ministries of John Wesley and George Whitfield. There is little evidence of this movement initially

29

having any impact on Baptist life, and it is perhaps surprising that it is hardly mentioned in Baptist records of that period.

Another matter of national significance was the concern of many people at the continuing attempts of the Stuarts to reclaim the British throne. This concern was raised to new heights during 1744-1746 when the rebellion begun in Scotland was carried down to England by Charles Edward Stuart ('Bonnie Prince Charlie') whose aim was not only to restore the Stuarts to the throne but to establish Roman Catholicism as the national church. Prayers of thanksgiving were offered in the churches for the victory at the Battle of Culloden in 1746, a victory which the churches spoke of as 'deciding finally the fate of the Stuarts and Popery'.

Despite the significant growth of Methodism in the 1740s, the Association records of this period indicate both a decline in spiritual vitality and in the number of members. The meetings regularly bemoaned the lack of godly living among members and a growing formality creeping into the churches. Although it cannot be affirmed with certainty, it could well be that it was this depressing picture that caused the Association to cease to function between 1754 and 1778.

Chapter 6.

# Rev Charles Whitfield 1770 – 1795

Many would maintain, justifiably, that the most significant person in Baptist history in North East England was Charles Whitfield, minister of the Hamsterley church from 1771 to 1821, so it is worth recounting some details of his life. But before doing so, it would be helpful to get a picture of the phenomenal growth of the Methodist movement in the North East during the eighteenth century, since Whitfield owed his conversion and early Christian development to the ministry of John Wesley.

John Wesley first visited Newcastle in May 1742, and within a year the Newcastle Methodist society had grown to over 800 members. His brother Charles followed up with an extended visit of several weeks in October of that year, and established several Methodist societies on Tyneside. Between 1742 and 1746 John Wesley spent 260 days in Newcastle and the surrounding area (almost one fifth of his time) and Charles spent 180 days. Within five years Methodism had become well established throughout the region. Several full-time travelling preachers were appointed by John Wesley, and the quality of their lives and work bore much fruit, particularly among the pit villages.

Seven months after Wesley's first visit to the North East, a Methodist meeting place was built in Newcastle, and part of the building was Wesley's residence and study. Newcastle was to become one of the three main centres of Methodism in England (the other two being London and Bristol). Within twenty-five years many Methodist meeting places had been erected throughout the region, and membership had become so large that it was decided to create many daughter circuits rather than have one enormous circuit based in Newcastle. One illustration of this growth may be seen in the Dales circuit (covering Teesdale and Weardale) which was formed in 1757. By 1770 it had twenty-seven societies and over 1000 members.

By 1780 there were over 52,000 members of Methodist societies in England, and it is reckoned that at least 25% of these were to be found in North East England. Between 1742 and 1790 John Wesley visited the North East on forty-eight occasions, some of his visits being of almost two months duration. The Methodist societies were well placed to take advantage of evangelistic opportunities, and this resulted in significant growth. When

John Wesley died in 1791 (by which time the worldwide membership of Methodist societies had reached almost 135,000), Methodism was the dominant feature of religious life in North East England, and this was to continue for many years.

During his lifetime, John Wesley and the Methodist movement were opposed by many people, including Anglican and dissenting ministers (among whom were the Baptists). The two main factors causing opposition by dissenting ministers were Wesley's Arminian theology, and his insistence that Methodism must not separate from the Church of England ('There will be no separation while I live; I am going to live and die an Anglican'). Regular entries in Wesley's Journal indicate that he was very critical of Baptists, always referring to them as Anabaptists. This critical view was reciprocated by some Baptists, and it is on record that some dissenting churches excommunicated members who associated with Methodists. Methodism attracted many people in other denominations who warmed to the spirituality and the seeking after holiness that characterised their class meetings. All the other denominations (Anglican, Presbyterian, Independent and Baptist) did not show great evidence of spiritual life and growth in the latter half of the eighteenth century, and it is a reasonable assumption that one of the causes of this was the appeal and attractiveness of Methodist spirituality.

Let us return to the story of Charles Whitfield. He was born in 1748 in East Blackdene, near St John's Chapel in Weardale. Shortly after the death of his father in 1761 he began an apprenticeship in Newcastle. He joined the city's Methodist society following one of John Wesley's visits there, and within a short time was accepted as a Methodist local preacher. Wesley recognised him as a young man of great promise and took a personal interest in him. He gave him volumes of his sermons and gave instructions that he had to have free access to the Methodist chapel and library.

It was said that in addition to doing a full day's work, Whitfield devoted five hours every day to personal study. As a result of his study of Scripture he began to develop his own theological views. On hearing him pray on one occasion, John Wesley said, 'Brother Whitfield has offered up a Calvinistic prayer'. As well as developing a Calvinistic outlook Whitfield became convinced of the truth of believers' baptism. As a consequence he left Methodism and identified with the Baptist church which met in Tuthill Stairs, Newcastle, being baptised by its pastor, John Allen.

In 1770 when visiting his mother in Weardale, he preached at Wolsingham. A member of the Hamsterley church was present on that occasion, and invited him to preach at Hamsterley, which he did on the last Sunday of 1770. When the matter of the church's pastorate was raised, he said he would favourably respond to a call to the pastorate if the church felt so led. Shortly afterwards he preached at both Rowley and Hindley, and in 1771 accepted the invitation to the pastorate of the Hamsterley/Rowley/Hindley church. The following year he took up residence at Hamsterley and was to remain there till his death in 1821.

While still resident in Newcastle, Whitfield travelled to Hamsterley to preach on 17 November 1771. Arriving at Witton-le-Wear, he found that due to flooding, the bridge over the River Wear had been swept away. Although only two miles from the end of his journey, he walked further down the river to the next crossing at Bishop Auckland, adding about twelve miles to his journey. He eventually reached Hamsterley, preached twice, returned that night to Newcastle, having travelled over seventy miles.

Charles Whitfield's early years saw the Hamsterley/Rowley church grow. Almost fifty new members were added in the first three years, and by 1774 there were over 100 church members, though the Hamsterley church services normally had attendances between 150 and 200. Although the first 25 years of Whitfield's pastorate did not see any great spiritual movements, the second 25 years were marked by a new spirit of confidence, resulting in revival and renewed missionary effort.

In 1784 Whitfield proposed that Hamsterley and Rowley become two separate churches. The two main reasons he gave were the considerable time spent in travel between the three congregations and the ill-health of Mrs Whitfield (she died the following year leaving three young children). The Rowley congregation sadly and reluctantly agreed to this proposal, and the twenty-two members formed themselves into the Rowley church, and that year Mr Ross accepted the invitation to be their pastor.

Whitfield revived the Association in 1778, but by 1784 it had once again sunk in abeyance. No reason for this is given, but it is very probable that one major factor was Whitfield's inability to give time and energy to it because of a combination of personal factors, not least the continuing ill-health of his wife. When Whitfield revived the Association in 1795, it was established on a solid basis, and from then on was to play a significant part in Baptist life, witness and growth.

Whitfield was not only a theologian, but interested himself in legal and agricultural studies, and his wide knowledge in a variety of subjects resulted in him having a prominent position among the people of Hamsterley and the surrounding area. In 1775 he had written a book, 'The Form and Order of a Gospel Church', and its wide circulation and reception resulted in him being highly respected by ministers and churches throughout the country.

In 1801 Charles Whitfield published a memoir of the Rev Isaac Slee, and it may be of interest to give some details of this man's life which merited the writing of his biography. Isaac Slee was minister of an Anglican church in Cumberland. In 1776 he had a spiritual experience which resulted in him leaving the Anglican church in 1779. He probably came to the annual meeting of the Association at Hamsterley that year and as a result identified with the church there. He was baptised by Charles Whitfield and received into membership. He ministered at Hamsterley and the other Association churches and became widely known as an able preacher. He accepted an invitation to be pastor of the Haworth Baptist church in Yorkshire and was ordained by Whitfield in 1781. Sadly three years later he died of consumption while still in his early thirties and Whitfield reckoned the Baptist cause had lost a pastor and Christian leader of great potential.

One of the Baptist congregations formed in North Yorkshire as a result of the itinerant preaching of David Fernie was in the village of Middleham, and Charles Whitfield visited the church twice yearly to give ministry. On one of these visits in 1792, Mr William Terry, a watch-maker from Bedale was present, and became convinced of the truth of believers' baptism. At this time he was identified with the Methodists, having previously been a 'ring-leader in iniquity'. He requested to be baptised by Mr Whitfield, and in January 1793 he and a friend came to Hamsterley and were baptised and received into membership. On the day of his baptism he preached at Hamsterley. Later that year at Bedale eighteen people formed themselves into a Baptist church and Charles Whitfield ordained William Terry as their pastor. Terry had a fruitful preaching ministry both in Bedale and many of the surrounding towns and villages, and after some years the Bedale church had over one hundred members. Right up till the time of his death in 1819 he continued to work as a watch-maker and devoted most of his free time and his income to helping the churches and furthering the work of the Kingdom of God.

Chapter 7.

# Signs of Growth 1795-1815

Largely as a result of the leadership and initiative of Charles Whitfield, the Association was revived in 1795. From this time onwards full records were kept of Association affairs and on the opening page of the minute book the following wording appears: "The Northern Association of Baptist Churches was begun in the last century, carried on by the churches meeting at Hamsterley, Newcastle-upon-Tyne, Broughton, Hawksheadhill, Rawdon, Pontefract, Bridlington and Hull, continued until about the year 1750. This was revived in 1777 by the churches at Hamsterley, Sunderland, Broughton, Whitehaven and Hawksheadhill and continued until the year 1783 when the last was held at Whitehaven. Another attempt is made to revive it by those churches of the Eastern District now meeting at Hamsterley, Rowley and Newcastle-upon-Tyne. May it please the Lord to smile upon this undertaking. Amen."

Although there were more than three Baptist churches in the North East at this time it would seem that the three churches at Hamsterley, Rowley and Newcastle agreed to begin with themselves, hoping and believing that other churches would join them in due course. Much of the proceedings of the 1795 assembly was devoted to defining the purpose of the Association and laying a good foundation for its future work. The messengers (as the church representatives were then called) agreed a statement of belief containing nine articles, and they affirmed they would receive any church into the Association which accepted that statement of belief. There is evidence that they had fellowship and contact with other Baptist churches in the region, even though these churches were not at the time members of the Association.

The annual Association meetings were either two or three-day events, and most of the time was devoted to worship, prayer and preaching, several of the sessions being open to the public. It is of interest to note that of the six preachers invited to speak at the meetings in 1800, three were Independent (i.e. Congregational) ministers. The minutes of the 1806 meetings state that a welcome was given to four Congregational ministers and it would seem that members from Congregational churches were encouraged to attend the public meetings.

An important part of each Assembly was the reading of a letter from the member churches in which they related how they had fared during the previous twelve months. Another feature was agreeing on the contents of an annual letter to be sent from the Association to the churches. The normal practice was to agree on a theme or themes for each letter and entrust the task of its writing to one of the ministers of a church in the Association.

The church at Newcastle had experienced mixed fortunes in the latter part of the eighteenth century. Shortly after John Allen, the pastor, moved to America in 1771 the church became divided and by 1780 was 'in a very languid state'. That year Richard Fishwick came from Hull to establish the Elswick Lead Works. He identified with the church at Newcastle and his presence seems to have brought new life to the church. He became an enthusiastic supporter of the Baptist Mission under William Carey, and gave £350 of the £700 required to purchase the building in Stephenson Street, North Shields for the new church there. In 1796    Thomas Hassell became minister of the Newcastle church and under his leadership the church saw significant growth. During his ministry a new chapel at Tuthill Stairs was opened.

In 1797 the revived Baptist cause in Sunderland was received into membership of the Association. The following year the members built a chapel in Sans Street, and in 1813 it was rebuilt with increased accommodation. In 1877 this fellowship amalgamated with the church in Borough Road, moved to new premises and became known as Lindsay Road Baptist Church. A meeting house for Baptists was erected in Monkwearmouth on the north side of the River Wear in 1818 to accommodate a church that had been formed in that area in 1808. In 1834 this church moved to new premises in Barclay Street and became known as Enon Baptist Church. For many years this church was in a weak condition, but things improved when the Rev E S Neale from Spurgeon's College became pastor in 1870.

In 1798 a Baptist church was formed in North Shields and the circumstances surrounding its formation are interesting. Robert Imeary was a young man from Aberdeenshire in Scotland who was travelling to London with a view to doing missionary work under the auspices of the London Missionary Society. Stopping en route at Newcastle, he attended a baptismal service at the Tuthill Stairs chapel conducted by the minister, Thomas Hassell, which caused him to question his views on baptism. He continued to London but becoming convinced about believers' baptism he returned to Newcastle and asked Thomas Hassell to baptise him and he also sought his advice about future Christian service. Some of the Tuthill Stairs members resided in North Shields, and Robert Imeary agreed to go there and undertake evangelistic work. God blessed his efforts, and a Baptist church was formed and he became its first pastor. In 1799 the assembly room in Stephenson Street was purchased and converted into a Baptist chapel. At the 1800 Assembly the North Shields church was received into membership of the Association. Mr Imeary died in 1814 and a tribute which was printed in the Baptist Magazine described him as one who was for 'many years the highly respected and beloved pastor of the Baptist Church, North Shields'.

At the 1798 Assembly a new Christian organisation was formed, called 'The Northern Evangelical Society'. Its objects were to unite the Independent and Baptist ministers of the region and establish itinerant evangelistic work, especially in areas where there was little, if any, gospel witness. The first meeting of this new body took place in Cumbria in August 1798 at which they decided on the areas in which they should work.

David Fernie had led the Stockton/Marton church since its beginning, and Valentine Short, who had been connected with the church for many years, took on the role of leadership on Fernie's death in 1789. In 1799 Thomas Sheraton, a Stockton born mechanic of distinction and founder of the famous furniture firm which bore his name, was invited to share the church's ministry with Mr Short. Charles Whitfield and Thomas Hassell conducted Mr Sheraton's ordination that year. Unfortunately the church lost both its leaders with the death of Mr Short in 1802, and Mr Sheraton's moving to London in 1804 and over the next few years the church declined. In 1809 Charles Whitfield of Hamsterley responded to an appeal for help from the few remaining members. He encouraged Rev William Hartley (then aged sixty-nine years, who since 1772 had pastored churches in Yorkshire and the North East prior to moving to live in Newcastle) to move to Stockton and help the church. He was accepted by the members as their pastor, a meeting place in West Row was established, and in 1810 the re-organised church was received into the membership of the Association, and the following year the church played host to the Association's Annual Assembly. Mr Hartley's pastoral oversight of the church continued until his death in 1822.

The 1790s was a decade in which mission and evangelism came to the fore in churches throughout the country. The Baptist Missionary Society was founded in 1792, and the Baptist Home Missionary Society in 1797 (the latter being the inspiration behind the Association creating the Northern

Evangelical Society). Other denominations formed their own missionary societies and organisations, and this all created a spirit of optimism about future growth. This prospect of growth was one reason behind the decision to make pastoral leadership the major item for consideration at the 1801 Assembly. The Association asked the churches to encourage 'young men of piety and talent' to consider seriously the work of pastoral leadership, and the church messengers agreed that on Saturday afternoons at 3 o'clock they would make this a matter of special prayer.

The influence of the evangelistic efforts of the Haldane brothers in Scotland was felt in Northumberland. Baptist churches were formed in the north of the county in Ford Forge, Wooler and Berwick-on-Tweed in the early 1800s, but none of these churches came into membership with the Association, since at the time of their formation they were modelled on the Scotch Baptist basis. The Scotch (not Scottish!) Baptists find their origins in Archibald MacLean who became one of the elders of a Baptist church shortly after it had been formed in Edinburgh in 1765. Believing that the Scriptures present a model of church life for all time, he introduced innovations into his church which were later adopted by other Baptist congregations. These included feet-washing, sharing in a love-feast and the weekly observance of the Lord's Supper. They rejected the idea of a trained ministry, believing that church leadership was a plurality of elders and not a single pastor, as was becoming the norm in 'English' Baptist churches. The Scotch Baptists placed great emphasis on evangelism and were strong supporters of the BMS. Their evangelistic endeavours extended into England and Wales, and in addition to founding several churches in the North East they established churches in London, Liverpool, Lancashire, Nottingham and Chester. By the mid-nineteenth century the movement began to decline and has now virtually disappeared.

In 1805 Dr John Fawcett, a leading Baptist minister in Yorkshire, formed the Northern Baptist Education Society in Bradford for the training of Baptist ministers. Later this was to become Rawdon College and then in 1964 it was incorporated into the Northern Baptist College in Manchester. The Rev (later Dr.) William Steadman became its first principal, and he was to prove a good friend and helper of the churches in the Northern Association, not only visiting the North East on many occasions, but providing students and pastors to help the churches in their work.

In 1807 Richard Pengilly was ordained as pastor of the Newcastle church meeting in Tuthill Stairs and his coming to the area not only marked the beginning of significant growth in the Newcastle church, but he was to play a major role for many years in Baptist witness throughout North East England. When he was ordained the Tuthill Stairs membership was 29. When he resigned in 1845 the membership was 209, and two other churches had been formed in Newcastle by Tuthill Stairs members.

In 1811 visits were made to the North East by three of the main leaders of the Baptist Missionary Society – John Ryland, John Sutcliffe and Andrew Fuller. They met in several locations telling how God was prospering the BMS work in India being done by Carey, Marshman and Ward. These visits increased the interest in and support of the BMS by the Baptist churches throughout the region.

At the beginning of the nineteenth century there was a growing desire on the part of many Particular Baptist ministers throughout the country for a national identity. In 1812 over sixty of these ministers (none of whom came from the North of England) met to discuss the formation of a national network, and the following year churches and Associations were encouraged to send representatives to a meeting which marked the formation of a national Baptist Union. At this meeting those present agreed twelve resolutions which formed the initial constitution of the Union. Beginning with a doctrinal statement, the resolutions went on to define the purpose of the Union, two main emphases being fellowship and co-operation in mission. Distance prevented the Association from having as active an involvement as other parts of the country, though a representative from the Association did attend its Annual Meeting in 1814. It was quite a number of years before the Union became a significant factor in the affairs of the Northern Association and its churches.

# Chapter 8.

# Enlargement and Development: 1815-1849

In 1819 Charles Whitfield was struck down with paralysis and was unable to continue his ministry both at Hamsterley and in the Association. At the Association Assembly that year tributes were paid to him in his absence, and it would seem that Richard Pengilly of Newcastle took over Whitfield's mantle and was to become the leading pastor in Association affairs for the next twenty five years. Also at the Assembly the church at Broughton in Cumberland was received into membership.

In 1820 Charles Whitfield invited David Douglas, a member of the Edinburgh Baptist Church and a student at Bradford Academy, to provide temporary ministry to the Hamsterley church. During that year he supplied the pulpit for four months, and in 1822 was ordained as pastor and served the church there until his death in 1849. He was to prove a worthy successor to Mr Whitfield, both in the ministry to the church and his active interest in the well-being of all the churches in the Association.

Charles Whitfield died in 1821 and his passing was widely mourned throughout the whole Baptist denomination. David Douglas pays a lengthy and fulsome tribute to him in his book, saying that for many years "he was the head, the heart and the hand of the Association". He had played a major role in the establishing of many Baptist churches throughout the region. In addition to his pastoral work he was the leading advocate in the North East for the national Baptist Home, Irish and Foreign Missions. He enjoyed fellowship with Christians of other denominations in his labour for the Northern Evangelical Society, an organisation which he was largely instrumental in founding in 1798 to unite all the Independent and Baptist ministers of the four northern counties in itinerant evangelistic work throughout the region. He was reckoned to be one of the finest Hebrew scholars of his day. As a tribute to his almost fifty years of pastoral labour, the Hamsterley congregation erected a stone in their chapel graveyard to honour his memory.

In 1823 William Leng, a student at Bradford College, was ordained pastor of the Stockton church and was to sustain a steady ministry of forty six years there in which he saw the church grow from twenty-six to seventy-three members. It is worth noting, however, that the church reported an average attendance of one hundred in a census of church attendance in 1835, and in 1840 the church built a gallery in its West Row building to accommodate increasing congregations. In addition to pastoring the Stockton church, Mr Leng kept three preaching stations open at Marton, Yarm and Middlesbrough. On four separate occasions he served as moderator of the Association.

It would seem that the Sunderland church ceased to exist in the early years of the eighteenth century, since the Association at its 1833 Assembly agreed to approach Dr Steadman of Horton College, the new name of the Bradford Baptist Academy, to seek the help of a student in re-establishing a church in that town. One of the Horton students, Mr Hoe, visited the town for a few weeks to help in this. The following year the Assembly encouraged each church to take a collection for the new Sunderland church and in 1835 the newly-formed congregation which met in Monwearmouth was welcomed into the Association as a member church.

The Berwick-on-Tweed church in 1832 enlarged its meeting house which had been originally erected in 1810. During these twenty two years five of its members had been called to full-time Christian work, one becoming a pastor of a Baptist church in London and four giving themselves to missionary service overseas. Although the Berwick church at this time was not a member of the Association, it actively maintained friendly relations with the Association churches.

Also around this time several other new buildings were erected. Among them were the Ford Forge church in Northumberland which had a new chapel built in 1844, and the North Shields church which opened its new premises in Howard Street in 1846. A new building was also being planned for the church in Sunderland.

## A Growing Association

In 1815 there were five member churches of the Association with a combined membership of 300. By 1849 there were sixteen member churches with a combined membership of 1287 and a Sunday School enrolment of 1650 children. In addition there were other Baptist churches with whom the Association had contact and fellowship but who were not actually in membership with the Association. Not only were these thirty four years a period of considerable growth, they were also marked by developments in Association life.

Although worship and preaching continued to be a major part of assemblies, the Association became increasingly active in several directions. It encouraged and gave practical support to pioneer evangelism and church planting. It passed resolutions on political matters and made petitions to Parliament. Since travel was becoming easier with the advent of the railways, it was more actively involved in national Baptist life. And because of the increase in matters requiring the attention and action of the Association, it appointed an Executive Committee to deal with these issues in the period between the annual assemblies.

At the 1820 Association Assembly, the Tottlebank church was admitted to the Association, and the following year the South Shields church joined, bringing the number of churches in the Association to eight, with a combined membership of 371. At the 1820 Assembly it was agreed that one session of all future assembles would be an 'Address Meeting' when all ministers would be expected to speak of the work of their churches to "stimulate the other churches in their labours".

In 1828 Parliament repealed the Test and Corporation Acts which for the previous 150 years had prevented Protestant dissenters from holding any but the most trivial forms of public office. At the Association Assembly that year this legislation was noted with thanksgiving, and the members agreed that a letter of thanks be sent to Lord Russell and Lord Holland who had introduced the bill.

The minutes of the 1829 Association Assembly noted that twelve pastors were present, four of whom were pastors of Baptist churches not in membership with the Association. A letter was sent to these four churches inviting them to join, and as a result the following year the churches at Middleton and Masham were welcomed as members. Several years after this, however, it was felt that due to distance it was deemed better for the Masham church to join the Bedale church in associating with the Baptist churches in the East Riding of Yorkshire.

Prior to 1829 the records of Association business and activities were to be found only in the minute book. Due to the growth and increasing influence of the Association it was decided that the minutes of all meetings of the Annual Assembly be printed and circulated to the churches. Soon this developed into an annual sixteen page booklet giving not only the minutes, but the annual statistics and a report of the work of each member church during the previous twelve months. The wide circulation of these annual reports created a greater interest and involvement in Association life by many of the churches and their members.

A bill was placed before Parliament in 1832 for the establishment of a new university at Durham, one of the first provincial universities to be formed, London University having been formed in 1829. The two main universities at Oxford and Cambridge had religious tests which limited entry only to confirmed members of the Church of England, and the Association agreed to petition Parliament asking that this restriction should not apply and that no religious tests should be required for admission to the new University of Durham. This request was not granted, and it was only eighty-four years later in 1916 that the University decided its theological degrees would be open to all without restriction.

In 1839 it was agreed to form three districts within the Association. The northern district comprised the churches at North Shields, South Shields, Newcastle, Sunderland, Rowley, Broomley and Shotley Field; the southern district comprised the churches at Stockton, Hamsterley, Wolsingham, Middleton, Forest and Brough; and the western district comprised the churches at Carlisle, Maryport, Whitehaven, Hawksheadhill and Tottlebank. The main object of this arrangement was for each district to arrange quarterly united meetings, one main purpose of these gatherings being prayer for revival.

Another significant decision made that year was to regard the Association as an Auxiliary of the Baptist Home Missionary Society. As mentioned earlier Mr Roe resigned as pastor of the Middleton church in 1835 to become secretary of this Society, and he was keen to use the Society's resources and personnel in the north. Thomas Pulford of Devon was appointed as an evangelist for the northern counties, and he began his work in Carlisle. He held prayer meetings at 5 o'clock every morning and preached every evening, and a church was formed in that town which within twelve months had grown to fifty members. He also made extended visits to the churches in Broomley, Rowley, Hamsterley and Bedale, and these visits resulted in many members being added to these churches.

At this time there were two Baptist denominations – the General Baptists and the Particular Baptists. The only major difference between them was that the former were Arminian in their theology, affirming that Christ died for all, whereas the latter were Calvinistic, affirming that Christ die only for the elect. Although all the Association churches at this time were Particular Baptists, the Association at its 1840 Assembly passed a resolution expressing the desirability of these two sections being united in one body as soon as possible. Although similar views were being expressed in other parts of the country, it was not until 1891 that the two bodies were merged to form the Baptist Union of Great Britain and Ireland.

Also at the 1840 Assembly there was much thanksgiving to God for the growth seen in most of the churches during the previous twelve months. During that year the combined membership of the Association churches increased from 560 to 740.

In addition to appointing an Executive Committee, as mentioned above, the 1841 Assembly agreed a constitution as the basis of its work. Two other issues that year were a resolution expressing strong disapproval of American slavery, and the decision to send a petition to Parliament protesting against the enforced levying of church rates on any who dissent from the Church of England.

By 1844 there were twelve churches in membership of the Association, with a combined membership of 976. The churches at Tuthill Stairs, Newcastle and North Shields were the largest, having membership of 200 and 205 respectively. A major discussion took place at that year's Assembly which resulted in a resolution strongly supporting "the severance of church and state by all lawful and peaceable means". The resolution stated that church establishment was "derogatory to the kingly character of Jesus Christ, injurious to the spirituality of his kingdom, and calculated to impede the progress of the gospel". This issue, and also that of American slavery occupied the minds of the messengers at several future assemblies.

By 1845 the five Cumberland churches which formed the western district were no longer in membership, having identified with the Lancashire Association. The only church outside the historic boundaries of the counties of Northumberland and Durham was the church at Brough in Westmorland, and this link was to continue for many years. That year there were thirteen churches in membership with the Association, but David Douglas identified another twelve Baptist churches in existence at that time which were not Association members. In all its affairs the Association regularly affirmed the independence of its member churches, but it would seem that some churches felt that their independence would be compromised if they formally identified with the Association, hence their decision not to join. The evidence suggests that this did not prevent friendly relations being maintained between Association and non-Association churches.

**New Churches Established**

In 1816, largely through the preaching of William Terry of Bedale, a church was formed at Boroughbridge, and Mr Darnborough, a resident of that town who had been baptised by Mr Terry in 1811, was ordained pastor.

Also in 1816, a second Baptist church was formed in Newcastle by twenty-eight members who withdrew from the Tuthill Stairs congregation. Their secession was due to a difference of opinon regarding the pastor's use of his time. These people began meeting in the Carpenters' Hall, and in 1819 erected their own chapel in New Court. That year Mr George Sample, a member of Tuthill Stairs who had been set apart for the ministry by that church, began a two-year course of study at the Bradford Baptist College, and returned to Newcastle to pastor the Carpenters' Hall church in 1818, with Dr Steadman sharing in the service of ordination.

The population of South Shields was growing at this time. Some of the members of the North Shields church resided there and under Mr Imeary, pastor of the church, meetings began to be held in the town. William Angus, one of the North Shields members and later the founder of the British Sailors' Society, took a great interest in this new cause, and in 1818 the Association applied to Dr Steadman to send a student to preach in that town. The work of the student, John Winter, met with success, and that year a church was formed and Mr Winter was ordained as pastor. Most of the founder members were residents who up till then had been members of the Baptist churches in North Shields, Newcastle and Sunderland. In 1821 the members had a new chapel built in Barrington Street. Unfortunately the early years of this church were marked by impropriety and division, and in 1823, as a result of differences between the minister and the deacons, the recently ordained pastor, Rev George Brown, withdrew with some of the members and formed a separate Baptist church meeting in Queen Street. For several years the Barrington Street congregation was in a moribund state, and efforts to bring improvement were short-lived. However, in 1840 reconciliation took place between the Barrington Street and Queen Street congregations, and Mr Brown became pastor of the re-united church. He served as pastor for one year only, and was succeeded in 1841 by the Rev James Sneath from Brough, who had done such sterling work in establishing the Westmorland Baptist Mission, and in Mr Sneath's seven year ministry at South Shields the church grew and became firmly established.

A second Baptist church was formed in South Shields in 1840 as a result of the work of two brothers, Bertram and Joseph Richardson. They had come from Bristol and began to preach in the open-air. A number of people responded to their preaching, and identified with them in their open-air work, but the necessity of an indoor meeting place to nurture these new believers was soon felt. Growth in their numbers meant they had several changes of meeting place in the early years, and in 1855 they erected their own building in Cambridge Street, and called it Ebenezer Chapel.

At the beginning of the nineteenth century, several residents of Wolsingham were members of the Hamsterley church, and in 1818 with the blessing of that church, they established their own meeting place in the town. After a few years of continued growth a fund was established to build a new church. The Baptist chapel was erected in the Market Place, and its opening in 1831 coincided with the ordination of the Rev R Thompson as its pastor, and the members constituting themselves as an independent church. After a few years due to persecution and harassment, largely by landowners and the clergy (an experience also shared by the local Methodists), meetings ceased to be held in the chapel, though members continued to meet in their homes. In 1840 the chapel was re-opened and the church re-established largely through the efforts of Mr Thomas Pulford, the Association evangelist, and from 1842 the church began to flourish under the pastoral leadership of the Rev E Lewis. In 1889 the church extended its premises, and in 1901 purchased the property adjoining its premises to accommodate its expanding work.

The Stockton and Darlington Railway was opened in 1825 to bring coal from the Durham coalfield to the coast for onward shipment to London and the continent. The limitations of Stockton as a shipping port were soon recognised and the Railway Company extended the railway line across the River Tees in 1830 and created a new sea terminus on land which up till then had been an expanse of salt flats. This was the beginning of the town of Middlesbrough, and with the discovery of a main seam of iron ore at nearby Eston, the coal and iron industries resulted in Middlesbrough becoming known at the time as 'the fastest growing town in England', reaching a population of 40,000 by 1870. In 1840 fourteen of the Middlesbrough residents were members of the Stockton church, and it was this fact that caused William Leng of Stockton to establish a meeting place in the town. The congregation originally met in Graham Street and called themselves the Bethesda Particular Baptist Church. In 1849 the church moved to West Street and in 1856 applied for membership and was welcomed into the Northern Baptist Association.

A third Baptist church was formed in Newcastle in 1825, meeting in Weaver's Tower. It took its rise from two members seceding from the New Court church who wished to establish a church modelled on the Scotch Baptists. It would seem that this development took place in a spirit of goodwill, since the secession was not due to any difference in theological belief, but on how church life should be ordered. As time went on the Scotch Baptists' over-rigorous discipline to maintain a pure church caused some churches to experience division and discord which eventually led to decline. Through time most of their churches went over to the 'English' pattern, and this was the case with the Scotch Baptist church at Weaver's Tower which re-united with the New Court church in 1848.

A church was formed around the 1820s which eventually became the fourth Baptist church in Newcastle. Its members originally met in the Cordwainers' Hall, but there are no extant records giving the circumstances of its formation. In 1835 they moved to a meeting place in Marlborough Crescent called Providence Chapel. In 1865 the Rev Wildon Carr of the Rye Hill church in Newcastle withdrew from Rye Hill with some of its members, and they identified with this church and it became established as Marlborough Crescent Baptist Church. When the Bewick Street church decided to build a new chapel in Westgate Road in 1886, the Marlborough Crescent members decided to discontinue their separate existence, and they identified with this new venture in the west end of the city.

Several members of the Hamsterley church had moved to Middleton-in-Teesdale to work in the lead mines there which were owned by Mr Robert Stagg. Mr Stagg became favourably disposed towards the Baptists and in 1827 at his own expense erected a chapel in Middleton for their use and shortly afterwards the Middleton church was established as an autonomous church with sixteen founder members. Initially the ministry of the church was maintained by students from the College at Horton (the new location of the Bradford Academy), and one of these students, C H Roe, was ordained as pastor in 1828. Mr Roe resigned in 1835 on taking up the position of secretary of the Baptist Home Missionary Society.

While pastor of the Middleton-in-Teesdale church Mr Roe worked with Mr J Sneath, a Baptist Home Mission Evangelist, in opening several new centres of witness. Mission stations were established in 1834 in the neighbouring villages of Eggleston and Egglesburn, and when a new building was erected in Egglesburn in 1872 the congregation there constituted themselves as an independent church. Also in 1834 the Middleton church built a chapel in

Forest, six miles north of Middleton, and began holding services there. That same year the church established a fourth Baptist congregation located in Brough, under the leadership of Mr Breame, another Baptist Home Mission Evangelist.

Around the same time two new churches in Cumberland were formed and became members of the Association. In 1834 a new chapel was opened at Maryport, and the following year another chapel was opened in Ravenglass.

The Brough church exercised a remarkable ministry in its early years. In 1835 the Rev J Sneath moved from Middleton to Brough and was ordained pastor. He, together with Mr Breame, travelled widely throughout Westmorland in gospel ministry. They established farmhouse preaching places, mission stations and churches, and the work became known as "The Westmorland Baptist Mission". A church was formed in Winton, and after meeting for several years in accommodation which was not wholly satisfactory, they built their own chapel in 1860. Another church was formed in 1840 at Whygill Head (a farmhouse near Little Asby) with eleven founding members. Shortly after this yet another church was established in Great Asby, and they met in a hired room until their own chapel was erected in 1863. It would seem that the Crosby Garrett church began as an Independent (i.e. Congregational) church but in 1856 the members adopted Baptist views and re-formed themselves as a Baptist church, and that year converted a large stable into a chapel. Some indication of the extent of the Westmorland Baptist Mission may be gauged from the fact that their preaching plan for October-December 1843 lists no less than fourteen preaching centres.

For almost 150 years, largely through the leadership of the Angus family, worship had been maintained at Hindley, a small village two miles south of Stocksfield, as a branch congregation of the Rowley church. In 1835 the congregation built a new chapel at Broomley, about a mile from Hindley, as their new meeting place. The previous year some of the Rowley members built another new chapel in Broomhaugh, near Riding Mill in the Tyne Valley. In 1835 the congregation at Shotley Field also erected a new chapel. The four congregations decided to divide into two separate churches, with one pastor having the care of Broomley and Broomhaugh, and another pastor having the care of the congregations at Rowley and Shotley Field. In 1851 yet another new chapel was opened by the Rowley church at High Gate, located between the village of Shotley Bridge and the rapidly growing township of Blackhill on the northern outskirts of Consett. As a result of this extension the church re-named itself as "The Particular Baptist Church at Rowley, High Gate and Shotley Field".

In 1840 the Northern Baptist, a monthly magazine edited and printed in Yorkshire, reported on a mission held in the Rowley and Broomley Churches led by Mr Thomas Pulford, the Association Evangelist. A prayer meeting was held every morning at 5 a.m. and a preaching service at 7 p.m., and this mission resulted in over sixty people being converted and added to the church, and over forty children added to the Sunday School.

In 1846 the recently constituted churches at Darlington and Hartlepool were welcomed into membership of the Association. In both places, however, Baptist congregations had been meeting for some years, and it is of interest to trace how things had developed there in the preceding years.

In 1809 a Darlington grocer, William Lightfoot, was baptised by Charles Whitfield at Hamsterley and shortly afterward opened his home for Bible study and prayer. In 1823 David Douglas, who had recently succeeded Charles Whitfield as pastor of Hamsterley, began public worship services in a room in Albion Street, and in 1831 this group was constituted as a Baptist church with William Lightfoot and William Heron being ordained as pastors. A few years later this church came to be in a very low condition due to some members leaving the district and others joining a local independent church.

However, with Darlington's growth as a town, new residents came to live in the area, among whom were Baptists from London, Newcastle and South Shields. These people sought to revive the Baptist cause and approached the Rev George Sample of New Court church in Newcastle for assistance, and meetings began to be held in 1845. Help was also received from the Rev Richard Pengilly, the former minister of Tuthill Stairs church in Newcastle who had recently retired to Yarm, and under his guidance a new church was constituted in 1846, and that year it was welcomed into membership of the Association. Later that year David Adam was ordained as pastor, and the following year a new chapel was built in Archer Street.

The first mention of Baptists in Hartlepool, then a small fishing town with a population of 1300, is in the 1820s, though practically nothing is known of them. The first clear record is the hiring of a schoolroom in 1842 for Baptist worship. This church had originally followed the pattern of the Scotch Baptists, but in 1845 it dissolved itself and its members constituted themselves into a new church based on the 'English' order, and the following year it was welcomed into the Association. In 1851 the church, which by then had sixty-two members decided to erect a chapel in South Terrace, and this was opened for use in 1852.

## Supporting Overseas Mission

Since the founding of the Baptist Missionary Society in 1792 and William Carey going to India in 1793, Baptists throughout the North East had kept themselves regularly informed of the work of the Society and gave it their financial support. It was felt, however, that support could be increased by the formation of a BMS Auxiliary in the North East, and this took place in 1818 largely under the leadership of the Rev Richard Pengilly. The Auxiliary comprised a group of people who committed themselves to making the work of the BMS more widely known and raising financial support. Called the North of England Auxiliary to the Baptist Missionary Society, in the first few years of its existence it established six branch societies centred in various churches throughout the Association. Most churches appointed 'corresponding members' through whom information about the Society could be made known to the churches. In addition to this, the Auxiliary arranged regular public meetings at which missionaries and Society officers were invited to speak.

The Auxiliary published regular news bulletins, and in its first issue it described the 'amazing' things that were happening in India. In the first twenty five years of the work twenty-five mission stations had been established, between sixty and seventy missionaries were employed and over 1000 people had embraced the Christian faith. The entire Bible had been printed in four Indian languages, the New Testament in another five, Scriptures were in the process of being printed in another sixteen, and plans were in hand for this to be done in another fifteen. Ten printing presses had been set up to produce all this. In addition to all this 7000 children were under instruction in schools set up by the Mission.

The first bulletin of the Auxiliary also indicated the personal and church gifts for the Mission given throughout the North East, and it is interesting to note that the second highest church contribution came from a Methodist church. The 1821 report reported that as well as gifts from Baptist churches, gifts had been received from eight Methodist, four Independent and three Presbyterian churches.

**Gifted Leaders**

The churches of the North East suffered the loss of a great friend and helper in the death of Dr William Steadman in 1837. For thirty years he had served with distinction as the first president of the Baptist College at Bradford (latterly moving to Horton). He made many visits to the region, taking an active interest in the pastoral leadership of the churches, and providing not only students for pulpit ministry, but overseeing the settlement of many of them as pastors.

Following Charles Whitfield's death, Richard Pengilly, of Tuthill Stairs, Newcastle, came to play a leading role in Baptist life in the North East. But he also played a leading role in the city of Newcastle, being active in matters of social concern as well as evangelistic endeavour. He was a founder member of the Newcastle Auxiliary of the Bible Society and the Newcastle Religious Tract Society. For many years he was the secretary and assistant treasurer of the local BMS Auxiliary. In 1834 he was appointed by the dissenting ministers of Newcastle to be their representative at a meeting in London with other dissenters throughout the country "to consider the Grievances of Dissenters from the Established Church".

During his long ministry at Tuthill Stairs, Mr Pengilly led the church to significant growth and saw five of the church members called to overseas missionary work and three members called to pastoral ministry in the United Kingdom. One of these was Joseph Angus who was to become secretary of the BMS and then president of Regent's Park College in London.

Richard Pengilly, who had been pastor of the Tuthill Stairs church in Newcastle since 1807, resigned in 1845, and George Sample, who had been pastor of the New Court church in Newcastle since 1818 was unanimously invited to succeed him. Ill health forced his resignation four years later, but during that period discussion began about the erection of a larger chapel for the growing Tuthill Stairs congregation.

In July 1849 David Douglas died, having been pastor of the Hamsterley church for twenty seven years. He had experienced personal sorrow with the death of his wife aged 31 years in 1822 after only seven months of marriage, and the death of his second wife aged 41 years in 1841. In addition, four of his children predeceased him, including his eldest son who was almost blind and whose death occurred when he was aged 14 years. Yet throughout his ministry David Douglas served well not only his own church but the wider work of the kingdom of God. He was a strategic thinker as is evidenced by his "Essay on the Nature and Perpetuity of the Office of Primitive Evangelist".

He felt that pastorates of a brief duration, which had been the experience of several churches, were not conducive to growth and argued that much more could be accomplished in Baptist witness were the churches prepared to learn some lessons from Methodists. His view was that "a stationary self-supported eldership, superintending, attached to local portions of independent churches, might easily co-operate with a moveable class of itinerants or evangelists, supported by the churches in general, and stationed periodically, by a general union of the whole of these churches". It was his opinion that this was the pattern seen in "the working of the Primitive Church". There is no evidence to indicate that this suggested pattern of church life was ever seriously considered by the churches of the Association.

One could say that the passing of David Douglas marked the end of one era in the life of the Association. He, Richard Pengilly and George Sample had for many years been the leading figures in Association life, overseeing its development and influence. These men had been well respected in all the churches, ministering regularly in various congregations and welding the churches into a fellowship that worked for the advancement of the Kingdom of God in the North East.

# Towns having Baptist Churches in membership with the Northern Baptist Association in 1850

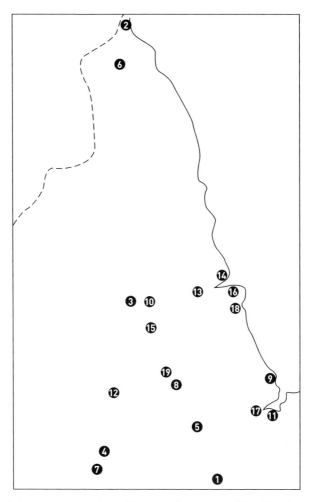

| | | | |
|---|---|---|---|
| 1. | Bedale | 8. | Hamsterley | 15. | Rowley |
| 2. | Berwick | 9. | Hartlepool | 16. | South Shields |
| 3. | Broomhaugh | 10. | Hindley | 17. | Stockton |
| 4. | Brough | 11. | Middlesbrough | 18. | Sunderland |
| 5. | Darlington | 12. | Middleton | 19. | Wolsingham |
| 6. | Ford | 13. | Newcastle | | |
| 7. | Great Asby | 14. | North Shields | | |

# Chapter 9.

# A Mid-century Snapshot of Baptist Life

It may be of interest here to give figures of denominational affiliation in the mid-nineteenth century. The government organised a first-ever religious census in 1851, and the main feature of this was church attendance on the last Sunday in March that year. The figures reveal that Baptists comprised the fourth largest denomination. The top five were as follows:

| | |
|---|---|
| Church of England | 4,939,514 |
| Wesleyan Methodists | 2,370,460 |
| Congregationalists | 1,191,978 |
| Baptists | 910,082 |
| Roman Catholics | 365,430 |

These figures record the number attending all services that day, so people who attended two services were counted twice. This means that it is impossible to state accurately the exact number of individuals affiliated to each denomination, but commentators at the time reckoned that the numbers indicated that around 50% of the population of England and Wales were in church on that particular Sunday.

Another piece of interesting information that indicated the growth of Baptist life is that the Registrar-General's census for 1801 stated that Baptists in England had 652 buildings and 176,692 sittings, and by 1851 this had increased to 2789 buildings and 752,343 sittings.

**Reports from the Churches**

When Charles Whitfield revived the Northern Baptist Association in 1795, one of the early decisions the delegates made was that two features should characterise Association life. One was that at each Assembly a report from member churches should be received relating how they had fared during the previous twelve months. The other feature was the preparation and sending of a letter from the Association to the member churches providing information and encouragement.

By the mid-nineteenth century these two practices were still being maintained, but a third means of contact between the Association and the churches had been introduced. This was the annual appointment of a deputation (usually comprising three or four persons) which would meet with the members of each church over the following twelve month period and then submit a report of their visits at the following assembly.

Space forbids a detailed look at all these reports and letters, so here we take a sample look at one of these years. This soon reveals that these reports were not simply concerned with the provision of information, but were the basis for positive action and the giving of assistance where necessary.

Reports of thirteen churches are included in the papers for the 1851 Assembly. The church at Brough had recently built a new chapel and the visitors were impressed by the wide ranging ministry of the pastor, Mr Kay, throughout Westmorland. The church at Darlington was unable to pay off an outstanding debt of £300 on the building, and the visitors opened a subscription list which immediately raised £100. The visitors to Hartlepool reported that a new chapel had begun to be erected, and they encouraged the other Association churches to give practical support. On the visit to Bedlington the Association deputation had attempted to heal a breach among the members, but had not met with success, and the visitors informed the Assembly with sadness that several members had subsequently withdrawn from the church. The visitors arranged a programme of pulpit supply to enable ministry to continue in that place.

Reports concerning the other churches reveal some situations that were experiencing real growth and others that were in decline. One church had seen many baptisms, yet this had not been reflected in membership growth. Another church had seen its congregation more than double during the previous twelve months. The reports on some of the churches include suggestions and advice given by the deputation to the churches to help them in their specific situations.

It may be worth recording the conclusion of the 1851 deputation's report. They write thus: "The Deputation have seen much in their visits for which to thank God and take courage; yet there is much in the state of our associated churches to call forth serious enquiry in the breast of every pious and contemplative mind. Most of them are few in numbers, feeble in influence, and some are even dependent for their existence upon the contributions of the Home Mission. Nowhere in the country, within the same geographical space, are there so many churches unable to sustain themselves; and some of these churches have existed for many years. There are also large Towns and Villages in the two Counties of Northumberland and Durham, in which we have no Baptist interest. Within the last fifty years, new Towns have sprung up; the population has been rapidly increasing; our ports have become more important; commerce has extended itself; and wealth has been accumulating; yet the Baptists, as a body, have not kept pace with this growing and improved state of things. Is it not time, Brethren, that as a denomination in these Northern Counties we seriously reconsider our position and solemn responsibilities?

"It behoves us therefore, everyone of us, for the sake of religion, for the sake of truth, for the sake of Christ, and for the sake of souls, to exert to the utmost our personal influence, to contribute more liberally of our worldly substance, and to pray more earnestly that the Lord would revive his work amongst us, and enable us to fulfil these high and noble purposes which in His Providence He has evidently designed us to accomplish."

By 1859 the practice of the Association appointing a deputation to visit all the churches seems to have been discontinued. It is uncertain whether this was as a result of the increasing demands such a visitation programme made due to the growing number of churches or whether it was caused by some other factor. Whatever the reason, it was replaced by each church sending a letter to be incorporated in Assembly papers in which was given a brief summary of how things had gone in the previous twelve months. On receiving these letters, the Association then decided if a deputation visit to a particular church would be beneficial. In 1859 the Association appointed a deputation to visit three churches whose situation was causing concern. The main purpose of these visits was to discuss and identify how these churches could be helped by the Association in the particular circumstances in which they found themselves.

**The Association's Circular Letter**

Since 1795 the Association Letter to the Churches was a general letter of information and encouragement, but in 1862 the Association considered it was an opportune time to develop its use further. They decided that each year these 'Circular Letters' (as they came to be called) would explore one theme at some depth. Each year the Assembly delegates would agree on a subject that was relevant to the life and work of the churches, and the composition of the letter was entrusted to one of the ministers. When its writing was completed it was printed normally as a twelve-page booklet and circulated to the churches for their consideration at the next Assembly.

The writers of these annual letters took their task very seriously and the Biblical expositions in relation to current events were often very thought provoking. When their contents were considered at the Annual Assembly meetings they would sometimes result in propositions for specific action being made by the delegates.

The 1863 letter by the Rev William Leng of Stockton was entitled 'Pastoral Efficiency', and focussed on how church leadership could be developed which would best help the churches in their mission. Also in 1863 the Association printed a second publication entitled, "The Baptist Denomination in the North of England". Its author was the Rev William Walters of the Bewick Street church in Newcastle who that year became secretary of the Association, a position he held for eight years. It is impossible to give here even an adequate brief summary of a very comprehensive document, but in reviewing the Association's history, Walters maintained that two main causes hindering growth were division and short pastorates. In suggesting steps the churches could take for growth he emphasised the need to foster the gifts and graces of the Holy Spirit in both personal and church life, the practice of family religion and a greater commitment to pioneer evangelism. To press home the last mentioned feature he identified many major population centres which had no Baptist witness.

The 1864 letter, also by Mr Walters, had as its theme, "The Relation of the Sunday School to the Church". He begins by recognising that Sunday Schools did not originate in the Christian Church as an outgrowth of church life, but rather they were the result of concerned individuals (such as Robert Raikes) organising classes where neglected children could be taught to read. Gradually, however, Sunday Schools were adopted by churches, and many soon recognised that next to preaching the gospel it was the most important work in which the church should engage. Walters maintained that a church was lacking if it did not have its own Sunday School, and this letter was in great measure a practical guide to churches in establishing and developing their Sunday School work.

The title of the 1867 letter by the Rev R Menzies of the Broomley church was, "The Consecration of Property to the Service of the Lord". This was not about church buildings, but about the attitude that Christians should take towards all their material possessions including their homes. The following year's letter focussed on Christian life style. Entitled "Christian Character as an Agency in the Conversion of the World", it maintained that Christians needed to live a life of conformity to Christ to give credibility to the gospel of Christ.

The 1870 letter again written by the Association secretary, William Walters, was to have significant practical consequences for the work of the Association. Its subject was, "Evangelistic Work within the Association". Walters focussed on the biblical office of evangelist, and argued for the Association to employ evangelists to work among "the masses of people who never enter our places of worship". He set out a management structure for such a scheme and proposed a programme of financing that would enable such a work to be undertaken by the Association.

As a direct consequence of this circular letter, the delegates to that year's Assembly unanimously adopted a resolution in which ministers and delegates "pledged themselves to promote, to the utmost of their power, the scheme for procuring and paying the expenses of two evangelists to labour in those parts of the Association as yet unprovided by Baptist churches". The Association secretary was asked to find a suitable evangelist for Crook, a rapidly expanding town due to the opening up of the rich West Durham coalfield, and the surrounding district at a salary of £100 per year. Churches and individuals were invited to contribute towards this work and the remarkable sum of £260 was received. When the Rev John Spanswick was appointed as evangelist under this scheme in 1871, his first sphere of service was with the recently formed congregation in Crook. The interest aroused by the 1870 circular letter was considerable and several churches approached the Association for the services of an evangelist in their area.

One of the churches that made an approach was Berwick, and when they promised to contribute half of the salary if the Association appointed an evangelist to work in their area, the Association proceeded with the appointment of another evangelist. Mr Henry Gray of the London City Mission was appointed to serve in North Northumberland and it was reported that his work was giving much satisfaction. On being made aware of the development of this evangelistic work, the Home Mission Committee in London agreed to provide additional finance which enabled the Association around this time to spend almost £400 in the upkeep of three evangelists and in giving grants to churches.

The circular letters for 1871-1873 covered these subjects: "Church Discipline"; "Infant Baptism and Its Relation to Other Errors"; and "The Aggressive Work of the Church". The 1874 letter by Mr H G Reed, a deacon of the Middlesbrough church, entitled, "The Position of the Baptists and

Their Relation to the Times", gives an interesting insight into public life in the 1870s. It gives the latest statistics as 2606 Baptist churches in the United Kingdom with 244,416 members, 62 British Baptists working overseas with the Baptist Missionary Society and 14,000 Baptist churches in the USA with a membership of 1,500,000. It highlights the social inequalities produced by the country having an Established Church and identifies areas in which Baptists could make their witness more effective.

### Petitions to Parliament

The subject of the 1869 letter, written by the Rev T H Pattison of the Rye Hill church in Newcastle was "The Political Obligation of Christians". Pattison maintained that a continuing obligation on all Christians should be "religious interference in all matters which lawfully affect us as patriots and citizens". The minutes of the annual meetings of the Association during the third quarter of the nineteenth century give ample evidence of the Association taking this seriously. During that period the Association made almost thirty petitions to Parliament on a wide range of issues, and also made personal contact with local Members of Parliament requesting them to raise particular issues with the government of the day. In one year they petitioned Parliament on four separate issues.

All we can do here is mention some of the matters that prompted these petitions, and they reveal the deep interest that was taken in political and other matters by the Baptists of that generation.

Education was a prominent subject of public debate throughout the nineteenth century, but it was not until 1870 that the Education Act was passed which provided compulsory primary education for all children (Scotland had incorporated this in law in 1696!). In 1812 the Government passed legislation in which they agreed to pay half towards the cost of erecting schools provided people in the locality raised the other half. The provision of education therefore was dependent on local concerned people who would raise money and serve as governors. Most of the schools established on this basis charged fees, many as little as sixpence a week, to enable them to remain financially viable.

However, as the nineteenth century progressed there was a growing recognition that there should be a national programme of free education for all children. The reason for the delay in government legislation was the objection of the nonconformist churches to the attempts of the Church of England to keep their control on education. The government accepted amendments to meet the objections of the nonconformists and eventually the 1870 Act became law. Between 1850 and 1870 the Association made six petitions to Parliament on this education issue, some expressing approval and some disapproval of particular aspects of the government's proposals. One particular matter that was to be a continuing cause of protest was that a proportion of the rates of all householders was used to support church (mainly Anglican) schools.

Concerned about the growing conflicts between nations, the 1851 Assembly petitioned Parliament to work for "a reduction in armaments by the British and Other Governments of the Civilised World". The following year they expressed their opposition to the Militia Bill which was then currently before Parliament. The militia was a body of citizens mainly enlisted to deal with emergencies of a local nature, and this bill meant that their future activities would be under the control of the Secretary for War.

Space forbids giving details of all other matters in which the Association petitioned Parliament, but listing some of them here conveys some idea of the breadth of their concern. These included alterations to the Marriage Law, the opening of public houses on Sundays, approval for the Burial Law that removed the exclusive right of parish ministers to conduct funerals in churchyards, a plea to cancel the existing patent for printing the Bible (a monopoly over which the Established Church had significant control), opposition to American slavery, and opposition to the government giving a grant to Maynooth College (a college for training men for Roman Catholic priesthood).

In addition to action by the Association, individual churches also took action, and all this revealed a deep interest in current affairs and a desire to apply biblical principles to national life.

# Chapter 10.

# Growing Optimism 1851-1874

At the 1851 Annual Assembly it was reported that fifteen churches were in membership with the Association with a total church membership of 1252. By 1874 there were thirty two churches with a membership of 3582. This period was one of the most fruitful in terms of church planting and church growth, even though some of the churches had to cope with difficulties and problems.

The two largest churches in the Association in 1851 were those at Tuthill Stairs, Newcastle, with 288 members and North Shields with 238, which was over 40% of the total membership of Association churches. The Tuthill Stairs chapel was no longer able to accommodate the numbers attending and the Association expressed the wish that the church build a new sanctuary "which shall be more in keeping with the improved architecture of the town". Two years later their new and much larger building was opened in Bewick Street, opposite Newcastle Railway Station, and congregations continued to increase. By 1859 the membership had grown to 347, and by 1875 it had increased further to 486.

In 1855 a letter was received requesting membership of the Association from a Baptist church of thirty six members in Witton Park. This church had not had any connections with existing Baptist churches, and it would seem that most members of the Association had been unaware of its existence prior to receiving the letter. The church was probably started by workers who had come from Wales for employment in the local colliery and iron works. The Assembly agreed that the church be sent a copy of the Association constitution, and if they accepted it they would be received into membership. When the church did indicate its acceptance at the following Assembly, for some reason the delegates deferred receiving them into membership. This uneasiness may be explained by events which took place a few years later.

Apparently the Association had received information from Wales that Zechariah Thomas, the Witton Park minister, was "a person not to be trusted". He had been having collections throughout England for the Witton Park church, and suspicions had been raised as to what happened to the money. Mr Thomas was invited to meet the Association Executive to discuss the allegations, but he declined. As a result the Association put the following advertisement in 'The Freeman' (the national Baptist magazine): "In consequence of information received, the Executive Committee of the Northern Association of Baptist Churches withdraw their recommendation and sanction from Zechariah Thomas, Baptist minister at Witton Park, who has been collecting money for the Baptist Chapel there". In addition, the 1862 Assembly delegates unanimously agreed the following resolution: "That until the Rev Z Thomas clear himself from the imputations laid against his character by the ministers from Wales, this Association withdraw from him and his church in Witton Park". There is no record of what subsequently transpired from this action, but it was not until 1872 that the church was received into membership of the Association.

Another church causing concern at this time was the Bedlington church. Division had weakened the church in 1851, and because of the difficult situation, the Newcastle and North Shields churches had been asked to provide ministry to the church. By 1856 the problems in the church continued to be unresolved, and that year the Association discontinued its responsibility for the church's pulpit supply.

Concern at the 1856 Assembly was also expressed about the Darlington church, when it was reported that the church had only fifteen members and was in "a low and unsettled condition and the acting members felt inclined to close the place altogether". The Association ministers agreed to provide ministry for the following six or seven months. Things had not greatly improved by the next Assembly and the Association wrote to the church urging them "to continued faithfulness and perseverance, and never to entertain thoughts of giving up". Mr J L Angus, an Assembly delegate, said that he would pay all expenses for Association ministers to continue supplying the pulpit. Fortunately the church did continue in existence and within a few years had reached a healthy state.

The church which had been formed in 1840 in South Shields as a result of evangelistic work of Bertram and Joseph Richardson grew under the pastoral leadership of Joseph until his death in 1858. On his passing, many paid tribute to his persevering and gracious work. In 1866 a student of Spurgeon's Pastor's College, the Rev Dr William Hillier (who had the Oxford degree of Doctor of Music), became pastor and under his ministry the church continued to grow, necessitating larger premises to accommodate the numbers attending. The church sold the Ebenezer Chapel, which they had erected in 1855, and in 1871 opened a new chapel costing £3,000 in Laygate Lane. Probably due to the pastor's connection with the Metropolitan Tabernacle in London, the church took the name 'South

Shields Tabernacle'. In 1873 the American evangelists, D L Moody and Ira D Sankey, conducted a week of special meetings in the new church building and this resulted in many conversions and continued growth of the membership.

In the early 1860s the churches were experiencing mixed fortunes. A religious census of the Association undertaken by a local M.P. in Sunderland in 1861 reported that the Sans Street Church had attendances of 217 in the morning and 341 in the evening, and the Enon Church 16 in the morning and 13 in the evening. While churches such as Bewick Street, Newcastle (now almost 400 members) and North Shields (almost 300 members) were seeing continued growth, half of the Association's eighteen churches reported very little change in their situations. Deputations were appointed to visit several churches that were in need of help, including Monkwearmouth, Sunderland and Hartlepool. The Association agreed to provide ongoing pulpit supply for some of the churches, and they agreed to arrange assistance for three years for the Middlesbrough church either through the Home Missionary Society or through the Association if the former was not possible.

In 1861 the Rev William Bontems, minister of the Hartlepool church, made connections with some Baptists living in West Hartlepool, and that year this group began meeting in a room in Brunswick Street which had recently been vacated by an Independent church. The cause prospered and ministry was given by Mr Bontems and friends from other Association churches, and in 1862 twelve founder members constituted themselves as the West Hartlepool Baptist Church. Following the resignation of Mr Bontems, the Rev John Charter became the West Hartlepool pastor in 1862 and he served the church for ten years. In 1864 the church erected a chapel seating one hundred and twenty people in Tower Street, and also purchased adjoining land with a view to erecting a larger building at a later date. Unfortunately when Mr Charter left the pastorate in 1872, for several years the church was "hopelessly divided and utterly discouraged", but in 1889 the Rev Alfred Curwood of Spurgeon's College began a twenty year ministry during which the church grew to be one of the largest churches in the Association.

The four churches at Berwick, Ford Forge, West Hartlepool and Bedlington were received into membership of the Association in 1862, the last-named having happily resolved the divisions that had characterised its life in the previous ten years.

For reasons not fully known the Middlesbrough chuch which had been originally formed in 1840 by William Leng as a preaching station of the

Stockton church was re-formed in 1857 and a new constitution adopted. Although Mr Leng retained an interest in the Middlesbrough church till he resigned as pastor of Stockton in 1869, in 1862 the church called the Rev W McPhail to the pastorate. Shortly after his coming, the church divided over issues relating to the constitution. Mr McPhail pastored the church in West Street for one year only, and in 1863 the Rev William Bontems replaced him as pastor. Under William Bontems the church prospered, and in 1865 the members began planning for the erection of a new chapel. After two abortive site purchases, a building was erected in Park Street and opened for worship in 1868, at which time the church had sixty members.

In 1870 the church called Mr W H Priter, a student of Spurgeon's College, to the pastorate, who at the time was only 20 years of age. He displayed a maturity and diligence beyond his years, and as a result of his labours the Park Street building soon became too small to accommodate the crowds attending the services, and attention was given to exploring a new place of worship. In 1874, by which time the membership had reached over 300, the church erected a new chapel seating 1100 people in Newport Road which was back to back with the Park Street building, and the church became known as Newport Road Baptist Church. Under Mr Priter's ministry the church continued to prosper, but very sadly a sudden illness resulted in his death in 1877 when he had not yet reached his twenty-seventh birthday. In his pastorate of seven years he had baptised over 500 people.

The members who seceded from the West Street congregation in 1862 began meeting in the Oddfellows' Hall and passed the following resolution: "That the individuals assembled at this meeting holding the form of Doctrine and Church Order adopted at the formation of the Baptist Church established in Middlesbrough in December 1857 ...... regard themselves as the Original Baptist Church, Middlesbrough". In 1865 this church applied for membership of the Yorkshire Baptist Association. In 1869 the members began meeting in premises in Stockton Street formerly used by a Welsh Baptist Church and renamed itself as the 'First (English) Baptist Church, Middlesbrough'. Four years later the church erected premises in Boundary Road and in 1875 appointed the Rev G W Wilkinson as their first minister.

In 1866 Mr William Stubbings purchased a former Wesleyan Chapel in Northallerton, and for twenty three years conducted two services there every Sunday. This was the development of a work he had begun as a young man in 1844 when, believing himself to be divinely prompted, he moved to Northallerton from Redford and began holding cottage services, visited the sick and dying, and opened a day school. He built a chapel in Brompton, about two miles from Northallerton, where he established a church with forty five baptised believers, and then opened a second chapel in Northallerton in 1866. He continued to minister in these two locations until his death in 1889.

For reasons that are unclear, following his death the congregations disbanded and both buildings were put up for sale. Since Mr Stubbings had strong General Baptist leanings, the church was not affiliated to either the Yorkshire or Northern Associations, but the secretary of the Building and Extension Fund of the Yorkshire Association, Rev John Haslam, became aware of the sale, and through the generosity of some of his friends, the properties were purchased, and in 1892/93 both premises were re-opened as a Baptist Church and Mission. By the end of the century the causes prospered and congregations in excess of two hundred were reported. At that time there were Baptist congregations in that area of North Yorkshire located in Northallerton, Brompton, Bedale, Masham, Boroughbridge and Dishforth.

The churches at Hamsterley and Wolsingham had a joint pastorate, and in 1863 due to differences of opinion about the pastor a rift had arisen both between and within the two churches. That year the Association appointed a deputation to visit the churches to seek to restore harmony. The Wolsingham situation was resolved amicably, but unfortunately the visitors reported that they had failed at Hamsterley because "the rupture was too deep to be removed", describing the church as "this feeble hill of Zion". It was only on the appointment of Rev J B Peel as pastor in 1869 that the church regained a sense of unity and purpose.

In 1861 the Hamsterley Church decided to seek help from the Baptist Home Mission in establishing a work in the nearby rapidly growing town of Crook and in 1869 they commended some of their members to this work. Two years previously, in December 1867, the Rev Peter Gibb, minister of the Wolsingham Church, together with some of his deacons, had begun holding services in Crook. Initially meetings were held in people's homes but from 1878 onwards they met in the Mechanics' Institute. In 1874 the members constituted themselves as a Baptist Church, and a few years later erected their own building in Grey Street. In 1890 the Rev A Graham Barton, minister of the Hamsterley Church, accepted the invitation of the Crook Church to be their pastor, and the church's period of greatest strength was during his pastorate of twenty one years.

In 1867 the Bedlington church withdrew from the Association, but that same year two churches were received into membership – a second church in Stockton (later Portrack) and the recently formed church in Jarrow. This Stockton church had been built by a Welsh Baptist Association to serve the spiritual interests of the Welsh steel workers who had come to Stockton for employment.

When Palmer's Shipyard opened in Jarrow in 1852 the population of the town rose rapidly and had reached 25,000 residents by 1881. Among the new residents were some Baptists. In 1864 the Baptist Union invited the Rev Charles Morgan to come to Jarrow with a view to establishing a Baptist witness in the town. His energy and enthusiasm resulted in the church being formed in 1866, and the following year a building was erected in Grange Road and the church was welcomed into the Association. The church made great progress and it was a great loss when Mr Morgan died in 1868. The church continued to prosper under the new pastor, Rev William Banks of Spurgeon's College. In 1873 a mission led by D L Moody and Ira D Sankey in Jarrow resulted in a great spiritual revival in the churches of the town, the Baptist church being one of these churches that greatly benefited. Their building proved too small to accommodate all those who attended, and this resulted in them erecting a larger building seating 700 on land adjoining their existing premises in 1880.

At the 1867 Assembly the Association agreed to support the erection of a second chapel in Darlington and South Shields (the latter being the South Shields Tabernacle which was opened in 1871). The Darlington church which met in Archer Street, whose poor condition was a matter of concern at the 1856 and 1857 Assemblies, had revived under the leadership of the Rev P W Grant, seeing its membership grow from fifteen to eighty during his pastorate of six years. He was succeeded as pastor by Mr J H Gordon in 1865, but sadly after Mr Gordon's arrival a serious division arose in the church, resulting in twenty nine members forming themselves into a separate congregation. Mr Gordon left the Archer Street congregation and became pastor of the new church.

It is uncertain which building project in Darlington the Association Assembly gave support to since both congregations in the town had building plans. The new church which had separated from the Archer Street church with Mr Gordon erected a chapel in Leadenhall Street. However, the Archer Street congregation under the Rev P W Grant saw significant growth, its membership increasing from fifty to over two hundred between 1865 and 1875. Among its members were quite a number of prominent professional people and business men in the town and from 1867 the church began to think about erecting a larger and more imposing chapel. Their hopes came to fruition when land was obtained in Grange Road and a new chapel seating 600 was opened in 1871. In 1865 the church had begun holding services in North Road Railway Institute, but in 1871 these were discontinued since the workers there now preferred to meet in the newly opened chapel. In 1879 the Leadenhall Street congregation decided to discontinue its separate existence and the members rejoined the Grange Road Church.

By 1867 the Association had twenty six member churches with a total membership of 2613, with 235 baptisms having taken place in the previous twelve months. Because of the growing work of the Association and the increasing expense this entailed, it was agreed that the churches would pay an annual contribution towards the Assembly expenses, depending on the size of their membership. Although the actual expenses of the Association were very minimal, it is interesting to see how the Association became increasingly involved in financial matters. Four pages of the 1871 Assembly papers were devoted to finance. Only half of one page was taken up by the Association's financial statement – it showed an income of £18.0.9 and an expenditure of £19.6.0. The remaining three and a half pages gave a list of contributors, both individuals and churches, to various funds, and details of how these funds were disbursed. Income for Home Missionary Work totalled £230 (including a grant of £60 from the Baptist Home Missionary Society). That £230 was used to give grants to seven churches to enable them to have a pastor. Over £167 had been contributed to the Evangelistic Work of the Association, and this money was used to pay the salary of and expenses of the Association evangelist.

In 1871 the Assembly welcomed plans being made to erect a place of worship at Consett. The formation of the church there was largely due to the initiative of the Rowley church. The  pastor of Rowley at this time, John Brooks, was a keen evangelist, and he established a preaching station in the rapidly growing town of Consett. In 1867 a Glasgow student, Duncan McGregor, was called to assist Mr Brooks in this work, and in 1869 the Consett Baptist Church was constituted under its first pastor, Mr Middleton. Also in 1867 a preaching station was established in Annfield Plain, but this never developed into a constituted church.

The work of the Baptist Missionary Society was continuing to expand, and this expansion increased the need for financial support from home churches. It was around this time that the practice began of having annual BMS deputation visits to the churches, and this arrangement was to continue for well over a century. Although the format of these annual deputations varied from year to year, on some occasions it took the form of a missionary home 'on furlough' who would spend two or three weeks in the North East and visit most of the churches. Also a decision was made at this time that each year an annual report of the Association would be prepared by the secretary and presented to the Assembly for discussion and approval.

Pease and Partners were the major colliery owners in West Durham, and since the Pease family were ardent Quakers, they employed seven missionaries to minister to their large work force. One of these missioners, J P Beel, accepted the invitation of the Hamsterley church to be their pastor in 1869, and under his ministry old divisions were healed and the church experienced a time of renewal. During a two week mission in 1874 forty conversions were recorded. Mr Beel had a further burden for nearby towns which were expanding due to the sinking of new mines. One town for which he had an especial concern was Bishop Auckland, and from 1870 onwards he regularly preached there in the open air. By 1871 a group of believers, the fruits of his evangelistic work, began to meet together in the town, and in 1872 this group applied to the Association for the services of an evangelist, similar to the arrangement that had recently been made for the neighbouring town of Crook. That year Mr Gray, with the consent of the Berwick church who up till then had been contributing half of his salary as an Association evangelist, moved from North Northumberland to Bishop Auckland and the following year a Baptist church was formed in the town. For many years the church met in hired premises and it was not until 1912, largely through the efforts of Mr A R Doggart, that they opened their impressive building.

In 1873 evangelistic meetings took place throughout the North East led by the American evangelists, Moody and Sankey. Many of the Association churches were involved in these meetings. At the 1874 Assembly it was reported that 709 baptisms had taken place in the churches in the previous twelve months. The Assembly passed the following motion: "That the heartiest thanks be sent to Messrs Moody and Sankey for the valuable services which, under God, they have rendered to the Churches of the Association".

At this time the influence of C H Spurgeon, minister of the London Metropolitan Tabernacle, was being increasingly felt in the North East. From 1855 onwards his sermons were published weekly and achieved massive sales worldwide. The proceeds of these sales helped to finance the Pastors' College which he set up to equip pastors and evangelists. Soon many of the Association churches began to look to Spurgeon to fill pastoral vacancies. For example, in 1874 the Crook, Wolsingham and West Hartlepool churches reported that their recently appointed ministers had come from Spurgeon's College. One interesting feature is the personal interest that Spurgeon took in the well-being of his students. When churches approached him he informed them of a minimum stipend he expected churches to pay their new ministers, and there are on record several instances in the Association where churches were unable to reach the figure stipulated by Spurgeon, and Spurgeon gave a personal donation to the church to make sure that their pastors would not be paid a pittance.

In the two-year period 1872-1874 the combined membership of Association churches had risen from 2666 to 3582 (a growth of 35%) and at the 1874 Assembly the committee reported that it "saw signs of coming revival and wished to prepare the churches to rise on its tidal waves by the arranging of prayer meetings for holiness and evangelistic meetings". Clearly a spirit of optimism was abroad, and although the times ahead were not without their problems, the evangelistic efforts of the churches were to continue to bear fruit for many years.

# Chapter 11.

# Further Development and Expansion: 1874-1899

One indication of the growing confidence within the Association was the Baptist Union's acceptance of their invitation to hold its Autumn Assembly in Newcastle in 1874. One significant feature of this Assembly was an address by Rev Richard Glover of Bristol who had been brought up in South Shields. Because of the growing expectations of the Union by the churches, he pleaded for a comprehensive reorganisation of the structure of denominational life. He advocated that the Baptist Union, the British and Irish Home Mission and the Baptist Missionary Society should all be united to form one body. This was to be the beginning of major developments in the Baptist Union, and the two Union secretaries, Rev S H Booth (1877-1898) and Rev J H Shakespeare (1898-1924), were to give a lead in introducing significant changes which were to create a framework which would serve the denomination for almost one hundred years.

The significant growth of the early 1870s resulted in the work of evangelism being high on the agenda of most churches. Growth in numbers was to be a continuing feature during the last quarter of the nineteenth century, but this growth brought pressure to bear on the Association to draw up guidelines so that the way in which they helped churches would be seen to be equitable and fair. One major issue was the annual giving of grants to enable churches to have their own full time minister. At this time there was a wide variation in stipends. Some churches paid an annual stipend of only £90, whereas some of the larger churches paid at least three times that amount.

During this period between ten and fourteen of the Association's churches were receiving help towards their ministers' stipend, help which came partly from the Baptist Home Missionary Society and partly from Association funds. Although it later came under the control of the Baptist Union, at this time the Home Missionary Society was one of several Baptist societies which operated independently of the Union and its committee considered each application from a church for a grant on its individual merits. Since some of the churches asking for help were paying stipends of £90 whereas others were paying £125, many saw a growing need to establish some criteria in the awarding of grants. When later the Baptist Union established an Augmentation Fund to help ministers and their families, certain criteria were agreed as the basis for the giving of all grants.

For many years the Newcastle churches had recognised the need of a Baptist witness in Gateshead. Sunday Schools had been started in 1823 and 1841, but it was not until 1875 that determined efforts were made to establish a church in the town. That year the Baptist Home Mission agreed to contribute £100 per annum for four years for a pastor in Gateshead on condition "that the Association take up work in the town with spirit and energy". The Rev Albert F Riley of Middleton-in-Teesdale was appointed pastor and under his leadership a church was constituted in April 1877 with fifty founder members, initially meeting in the Mechanics' Institute, and later that year the foundation stone was laid for a building on the corner of Gladstone Terrace and Durham Road. Within two years the membership had increased to 117. Mr Riley pastored the church until 1894, and during his ministry the church became a significant witness in the town. To accommodate all those attending the services, a gallery was added to the building increasing seating accommodation to 800. Mr Riley not only had an effective ministry in Gateshead, but became a leading figure in the work of the Association.

By 1875 the Bewick Street church in Newcastle had 486 members, and at this time two key features of its life were evangelism and prayer meetings for an outpouring of the Holy Spirit. The church was involved with the Moody and Sankey missions, and had several mission stations throughout the city served by a team of evangelists. The majority of members lived some distance from the Bewick Street church (which was located opposite Newcastle Central Station), and in 1883 the church accepted an offer of £15,000 for the property from the River Tyne Improvement Commissioners, and decided to use the proceeds to establish two churches – one in the east and one in the west of the city. Prior to this the church in Marlborough Crescent had considered moving to a location higher up the Westgate Road, and when they learned of the plans of the Bewick Street congregation, the two churches agreed to unite, creating a church with 539 members. The Marlborough Crescent minister became an associate minister of the Bewick Street church and four of their deacons became members of the Bewick Street diaconate. Following the purchase of the Bewick Street building, services were held in the Marlborough Crescent premises until the new building in Westgate Road was opened in 1886 seating 850 persons. The church in the east of the city was located in Osborne Road in the Jesmond district, and their building was opened in 1887. 131 of the Bewick Street members became the founding members of the Jesmond church, and the remainder identified with the church in Westgate Road. Shortly after the formation of the Jesmond church, their members accepted responsibility for the Byker Mission which had been established by the Bewick Street church and which eventually became Heaton Baptist Church.

Twenty six residents of Spennymoor who were members of the Wellington Street church in Stockton were encouraged by the Stockton minister to form a church in their own locality, and as a result the Spennymoor church came into being in 1876. They purchased an old Wesleyan Chapel for their meeting place, and the Association helped them in the settlement of their first minister, Rev M Morris. By 1879 the membership had increased to fifty five, and the church became a well-established feature in the town.

The Baptist church which had met in Barrington Street, South Shields, since 1821 began to look for a site for new premises in 1864 since due to the expansion of the town their existing building was becoming an island in a commercial area. One or two possibilities were explored without success, but in 1876 land was purchased in Westoe Road, and their new building seating 750 people and costing £6,000 was opened in 1881. The imposing new building was opened by the Rev Richard Glover, a native of South Shields, and over 650 people attended the event. At this time the church had 180 members and 328 Sunday School scholars, and within three years of the opening of the new building membership had grown to 205. The Rev Walter Hanson was minister of the church from 1862 to 1886 (during which time the population of South Shields grew from 35,000 to 75,000) and for fourteen of these years he was secretary of the Association.

The Rev Ernest Mason succeeded Walter Hanson as pastor of the Westoe Road church, and in 1891 a difference arose between him and the officers of the church on the matter of open and closed membership. Up till this time membership of this church was confined to those who had been baptised as believers by immersion, but Mason felt membership should be open to all believers. The minutes of the church meeting at this time were written in such a way to avoid giving offence, but from other sources it would seem that Mason was an authoritative person who did not feel bound by the church rules nor by decisions made at deacons' and members' meetings. The situation became so acute that he resigned the pastorate and took with him a substantial minority of the membership who sympathised with his position and formed a new church in the town. In 1895 they erected their own premises in Imeary Street and named themselves the Emmanuel Church. They applied to join the Northern Baptist Association in 1896 and after several committee meetings and some reservations (the Association minutes refer to it as the South Shields Free Baptist Church) they were welcomed into membership. It would seem that this division between these two South Shields churches was marked more by sadness than bitterness, because shortly after the division the two churches worked happily together in joint projects, not least when they co-operated in hosting the Association's Annual Assembly in South Shields in 1898. The Emmanuel church prospered under the pastorate of Mr Mason, reaching a membership of almost 200 by 1910, but when he left the church declined, and for many years struggled to survive. The cause eventually closed in 1953 and the few remaining members were welcomed back in the Westoe Road Church.

Although Kirkby Stephen was one of the locations included in the 1843 preaching plan of the Westmorland Baptist Mission, it would appear that this did not become a permanent congregation, since records say that the first meeting of the Kirkby Stephen Church was held in 1885 led by the Rev G Macdonald and friends from Crosby Garrett. The church did become well established, and in 1891 the members were able to erect their own chapel and schoolroom.

During the period of the Moody and Sankey missions in the 1870s many members were being added to the churches, but there was one disturbing feature in the information provided by the churches which the Association felt necessary to address. At the 1877 Association Assembly a total of 3679 members was reported with 461 members having been welcomed in during the previous twelve months. But the returns from the churches also revealed that in that same twelve month period 483 names had been deleted from the church rolls of which only 168 were due to death or removal. A resolution was agreed at the Assembly that all churches be informed that the Association was concerned at the large number of lapsed members that were being erased from church rolls, and urged the churches to give greater pastoral care to prevent this situation being repeated year after year.

The Newport Road church in Middlesbrough during the 1870s attracted many people, among whom were a group from South Bank, an expanding township three miles east of Middlesbrough, of whom twenty five became members of the Middlesbrough church. Some members of this group approached William Priter about the formation of a Baptist mission in South Bank, and in 1875 meetings began to be held there. Mr Priter invited Mr George Davies who lived in North Ormesby to oversee this work, and under his leadership the mission prospered. Though documentary evidence is scanty, it would seem that by 1877 the South Bank congregation (with an

73

# Number of churches in membership with the Northern Baptist Association during the Nineteenth Century

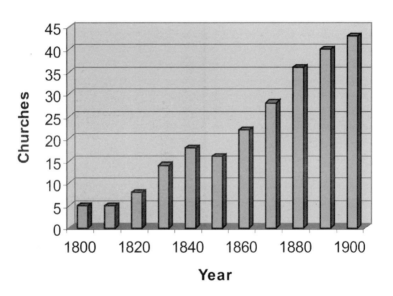

## Number of churches in membership with the Baptist Union during the Nineteenth Century
(estimated figures for 1800-1860)

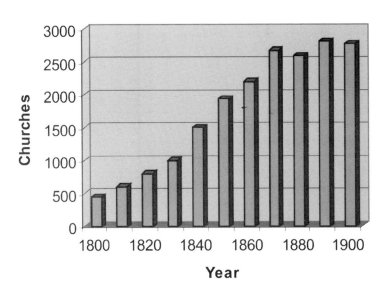

average Sunday attendance of 100) was established as an independent church and they appointed their own deacons.

The following year Mr Davies, who had a full-time daily job, felt the time had come for him to relinquish leadership and for the church to appoint a full-time minister. In 1879 a student of Spurgeon's College, Gad Pring, was inducted as pastor, by which time the church had eighty six members. Unfortunately differences arose within the church resulting in Mr Pring resigning in 1881. Shortly after this another student from Spurgeon's College, Herbert Atkinson, was appointed pastor, and sadly, though not of his making, differences arose once again within the membership which adversely affected the life of the church. It was not until the early 1890s when the Rev D M Pryse became minister that the church entered into a period of stability and growth. Since its formation the church had met in rented property, and although discussions began in 1897 about the church having its own building, this was not realised until 1906 when at a cost of £3200 the chapel in Redcar Road East was opened.

It was reported at the Association Assembly in 1878 that some young men in the Newport Road church in Middlesbrough had rented a hall in North Ormesby and had begun holding services there. By 1884 this work was established as a mission of the Newport Road church, and in 1890 they acquired a former Wesleyan Chapel as their meeting place, and made several additions and adaptations to the premises. This work at North Ormesby continued as a mission of the Middlesbrough church for over sixty years, and was only established as an independent church in 1953.

At the same time as work began in North Ormesby, some members of the Newport Road church established a mission in Cargo Fleet, and although it never became an independent church, the cause became strong enough for them to appoint their own minister in 1894. In 1904 the members decided to identify with the Wesleyan Methodists, and thereafter it became a Wesleyan church in the local Methodist circuit.

Another development from the Newport Road church, though sadly this was due to division in the church, was the resignation of ninety six members in 1886, most of whom identified with a new mission which the church had recently established. With such an influx of new workers, the members formed themselves into an independent church and erected a new church building in Marton Road, which seated over 500 persons. When they began using their new premises in 1889 they had 122 members on the church roll.

As mentioned earlier, the members who seceded from the West Street church in Middlesbrough in 1862 eventually erected their own building in 1873 in Boundary Road. At this time, however, many people including some of the members were moving from the area to the new housing developments at Linthorpe, and they decided in 1887 to buy land on Linthorpe Road and relocate their chapel there. They erected their new building costing £3000 in 1888, and in 1898 renamed themselves as Immanuel Baptist Church.

Yet another development in the Cleveland area occurred when about 1892 some of the members of the South Bank Church who lived in Redcar began holding meetings in that town with some ex-Methodists. Information about this group is very limited, but it was well into the twentieth century before it became established as Redcar Baptist Church and the members erected their own building in Park Avenue.

The population of South Stockton, later known as Thornaby, was expanding, and members of the Young Men's Bible Class in the Wellington Street church in Stockton began preaching there in 1880. Their first meeting room soon proved too small, and the following year they began holding their meetings in the Gaiety Concert Hall. Also that year this group called their own minister, Rev Henry Windsor, and formed themselves into a Baptist church with thirty seven founding members. In 1883 the church erected its own building.

Elsewhere in the North East the desire to expand Baptist witness at this time was evident. The usual practice was for churches to establish preaching stations or missions in new areas by hiring a suitable hall where regular meetings could be held. The churches would be fully responsible for these new ventures by appointing some of their members to organise and oversee their affairs. In 1877 the Darlington church opened a preaching station at Shildon and the Tyneside churches established missions at Hebburn Quay and Byker. In 1878 the Association began making enquiries about establishing Baptist missions in Hebburn, Wallsend, Willington Quay and Blaydon. In 1881 the Bishop Auckland church reported that it was holding meetings in some of the growing pit villages surrounding the town.

In the 1870s several members of the Rowley church came to live in Waterhouses, a small village one mile west of Esh Winning, and they identified with the nearest Baptist church which was in Crook. In 1877 they decided to establish a mission of the Crook church in their area and their first meetings were held in the British School in Esh Winning. In 1881 it was constituted as an independent church, and within two years they had opened preaching stations in Langley Park and Ushaw Moor. That same year they called the Rev R W Dobbie to the pastorate of the three congregations, which came to be known as the Waterhouses Group. In 1884 a letter from the Waterhouses church was received by the Association asking it to recognise it as a Union Church, but there was also a letter from a considerable number of the members opposing this action and asking the Association to send a deputation to discuss the measures that were being adopted to broaden the basis of the church. In the extant documents relating to this matter there is no clear definition of what constitutes a Union Church, but the most likely explanation is that it was a Baptist Church that was willing to receive members from other denominations without requiring them to change their views on certain matters. The Association felt this was too grave a matter for a hasty decision and asked the church to hold matters in abeyance for twelve months.

However, within six months the situation had deteriorated, and to try and resolve the impasse the Association advised Mr Dobbie to resign as pastor. After a few weeks' consideration he acted on the Association's advice, but a church meeting was held at which it was resolved that Mr Dobbie's resignation be withdrawn, and apparently Mr Dobbie continued as pastor for a further two years. The Rev George Macdonald succeeded him as pastor in 1887, but two years later he wrote a letter of personal resignation from the Association and shortly afterwards he left the church. From the limited information available it would seem that around this time two issues were exercising the minds of members in several churches, of which the Waterhouses church was an example.

One issue was whether people who have not been baptised as believers should be admitted to membership of a Baptist church. Those favouring both 'open' and 'closed' membership had their strong and vocal advocates. Several churches reported serious divisions in drawing up or revising their constitutions, and it was the matter of membership that was at the heart of the difficulties. The second issue, and it would seem that this was the main reason for Mr Macdonald's resignation from the Association, was his belief that some of the ministers in the Association were adopting the emerging liberal theology. Liberal theology was prominent in European Protestantism for half a century till the First World War. It had its roots in Germany, and some of its main features were a questioning of the authority and trustworthiness of Scripture, a sceptical view of the supernatural, a denial of penal-substitutionary views of the atonement, and a belief that mankind was moving spiritually upward and his moral progress will establish the kingdom of God on earth. No Association documents spell out this theological viewpoint, so there is no way we can come to any judgment about how much influence it had within the Association.

Shortly after this unsettling period the Waterhouses Group experienced what they described as a remarkable time of revival. A young Scots girl, Miss Carley, led a series of meetings in 1891 which saw many people come to faith in Christ, and this experience not only enlarged the church membership but injected the church with a new spirit. For several years afterwards Miss Carley made regular visits to the church engaging in teaching and evangelism, and blessing continued to attend her ministry.

The original meeting place of the Esh Winning congregation was a house in Durham Road which had been remodelled and transformed to become a chapel seating 200 people. By 1893, largely as a result of Miss Carley's ministry, the need for larger accommodation was recognised, but it was not until 1902 that a new imposing building was erected on the original site. In 1908 the church enlarged the chapel gallery and vestibule.

Members of the Esh Winning church began holding services in Langley Park, a village three miles away in 1881. In 1893 the members who lived in Langley Park erected their own chapel, but it was not until 1919 it was constituted as an independent church.

Around the same time as services began in Langley Park, the Esh Winning church commenced a work in Ushaw Moor two miles away. Meetings began to be held in a small hut, but this soon proved too small and the local mine owners offered the church the use of a larger building. Eventually the congregation erected their own chapel which was opened in 1897 and the schoolroom was added in 1925. Like Langley Park, the Ushaw Moor mission became an independent church in 1919. Even after Langley Park and Ushaw Moor became independent churches they maintained close fellowship with the Esh Winning church, and the three churches became known as the Waterhouses Group of Baptist Churches.

In 1887 two young ladies, Miss Carley, who as mentioned above was later to be a means of great blessing to the Esh Winning church, and Miss Sloane, conducted a month's "Revival Services" at the Egglesburn Church in Teesdale and six weeks of similar meetings at the nearby Middleton Church. As a result of these meetings, sixty two people were baptised and added to these two churches, and many were also added to the local Wesleyan and Primitive Methodist Churches. It is of interest that these two lady-evangelists were baptised as believers at the same time as the new converts.

The same year that Mr Macdonald of the Esh Winning Church resigned from the Association (1889), a letter from the Rev T L Edwards, minister of the Wellington Street Church in Stockton, was received by the Association in which he identified with Mr Macdonald and his concern about what he described as 'the new theology'. His letter informed the Association that he and his church were withdrawing from the Association since "the new theology has been making considerable headway among us and has taken deep root in the Northern Baptist Association ministry". As one response to this, the Association committee agreed a resolution to be put to the next Annual Assembly affirming that "we are earnestly united in preserving the great and vital principles of evangelical Truth". The fact that this proposal was agreed by six votes to four would suggest that there was division among the committee members as to the need to make such a statement. Although the questions of theological belief caused division the records of the Association at this time do not give details of any specific beliefs that were at issue apart from the general one about the authority and trustworthiness of the Bible.

A factor that influenced this unease was the withdrawal of C H Spurgeon and his church in London from membership of the Baptist Union. During the 1880s Spurgeon came to the view that some Baptist ministers were departing from traditional evangelical truth. Early in 1887 two articles appeared in 'The Sword and Trowel', Spurgeon's widely-circulated magazine, entitled "The Down Grade", and in later editions of the magazine that year Spurgeon used the term 'Down Grade' to describe the position of certain unnamed Baptist ministers who in his view were advocating "a new religion". The fact that no discussion of this issue took place at the autumn meetings of the Baptist Union resulted in Spurgeon withdrawing from the Union in October 1887. The following spring, however, on 23 April 1888 the Baptist Union Assembly agreed a 'Declaratory Statement' affirming doctrinal truth which closely resembled the doctrinal basis of the Evangelical Alliance. Many felt that this action would pave the way for Spurgeon to rejoin the Union, but this did not happen.

Inevitably Spurgeon's action was widely reported and since a number of pastors of churches in the North East had been trained at Spurgeon's College, it was inevitable that they consider seriously their own position. The majority of pastors, whether Spurgeon trained or not, adopted the view, a view which was reflected nationally, that while they were sympathetic to Spurgeon's position, they felt they should stay within the Association and Union and face the issues raised rather than withdraw. Some, however, did withdraw, one of which was the Wellington Street church in Stockton.

In 1889 a student from Spurgeon's College, Alfred Curwood, became pastor of the West Hartlepool church. Mr Spurgeon informed the church that he did not wish Mr Curwood's stipend to be less than £100 per year, and he gave a personal gift to the church to enable this amount to be paid. It is worth noting that Spurgeon followed this generous practice with several churches in the north-east whose pastors came from his college. For about thirteen years prior to Mr Curwood's settlement at West Hartlepool, the church had gone through a series of problems and met in a variety of locations, but under Mr Curwood it entered a period of growth and stability, with 231 members being added to the church during the first ten years of his ministry. A new permanent building seating five hundred people was opened in Tower Street in 1890, and in 1902 the schoolroom was enlarged since the Sunday School had grown from eighty to five hundred children, and a new Lecture Hall built. In 1892 Mr Curwood raised the issue of starting a second Baptist church in the growing town, but this possibility lay dormant for ten years. In 1899 the Baptist Union launched an appeal for £250,000 for a "Twentieth Century Fund", half of which was to be used for church extension. The appeal figure was reached in 1902, and a grant from this fund enabled a mission to be eventually established which in the course of time became Oxford Road Baptist Church. Mr Curwood resigned as pastor of the Tower Street church in 1908 due to health reasons, but in his ministry of twenty years he had welcomed over 400 people into the membership of the church and left a church which had become a strong evangelical witness in the town.

In 1883 the Association received a request from the Yorkshire Baptist Association to meet them to consider denominational work in Cleveland. The request for this meeting arose because a Middlesbrough Baptist church which met in Bernastay Road had applied for membership of the Yorkshire Association. When the two Associations did meet they agreed to suggest to the Bernastay Road church that they join the Northern Association in common with the other Cleveland churches, but the church was unwilling to take this step and persisted in their application to the Yorkshire Association. There are virtually no extant records of this church and in the early twentieth century it does not appear in the list of churches belonging to the Yorkshire Association.

The theological differences highlighted by C H Spurgeon's withdrawal from the Union continued to surface. One particular situation in 1891 which did affect the churches was the Association committee giving the view that the Rev Walter Walsh, minister of the Rye Hill (formerly known as New Court) church in Newcastle was 'expressing sentiments that caused real concern to the committee'. The committee made a two-fold response. They decided that no further Association meetings would be held in Rye Hill Chapel and they re-affirmed that 'the Association held what are commonly called Evangelical Views'. Some felt that the committee should have taken more decisive action even expulsion, and this resulted in letters of resignation being received from one or two ministers and churches in the Association. One church taking such action was Jarrow, and the reason they give in their letter is that the Rye Hill church's minister was compromising "Christ and Him Crucified" as the world's only hope for salvation. Although information is scant, it would seem that the issue resolved itself when Walsh resigned as minister of Rye Hill church in 1897 on becoming minister of the Gilfillan Memorial Church of Scotland in Dundee. Interestingly, on his departure the Association placed on record and sent a letter thanking him for his services in the causes of education, temperance and the social improvement of the working classes.

Another issue that was faced in 1891 related to finance. Growth during the 1870s and 1880s had resulted in many churches embarking on ambitious building programmes to accommodate growing congregations and also in the felt need to appoint a full-time minister. Some of the churches overstretched themselves financially and as a consequence became burdened with debts they were unable to repay. The Association was becoming overwhelmed with appeals from these churches for financial help, and they were unable to respond to many of the requests. The Association committee spent many hours deciding how best to share what was available. That year grants were given to thirteen churches, after which the Association itself was left with a debt of £130, but even that fact left some of the churches dissatisfied with what they had received. One church invited a minister and then approached the Association for substantial help in paying his stipend, but the Association declined to help because the church had not consulted the Association prior to issuing the invitation to the pastorate. All this was making it abundantly clear that the Association urgently needed to formulate, with all the churches' approval, some kind of agreed policy in the giving of grants to churches. As an initial step they appointed an Association Financial Committee, and agreed that they would only consider applications for grants when they were accompanied by a report of the church's work in the previous twelve months which had been passed by a church meeting. From 1895 onwards they agreed that financial support for ministry would be given only to those churches whose ministers were on the accredited list of the Baptist Union.

A surprising omission in the Association records for 1892 is the absence of any reference to the union of the General and Particular Baptist denominations that year. As mentioned in chapter eight, there were two Baptist denominations in the country – the General and Particular Baptists – and although the possibility of a union between them had been discussed since the 1830s, no definite action had resulted. Negotiations that eventually led to union were caused indirectly as a result of a letter from the Church of England which the Baptist Union received in 1889. In the letter the Archbishop of Canterbury indicated that the Church of England was ready to discuss with other denominations what steps could be taken to bring about closer relationships and perhaps eventually organic unity. The reply agreed at the Assembly of the Baptist Union that year was largely a statement of Baptist principles, but it also suggested that steps towards closer co-operation rather than a conference on the subject of reunion would be the better course of action at that time.

The raising of this issue, however, prompted many at that Assembly to express the view that the time had come to work towards Baptist unity, and the delegates agreed to begin formal negotiations with a view to the full union of the two Baptist denominations. After two years of negotiations it was agreed that the General Baptist Association would be dissolved and its member churches affiliated to the existing Particular Baptist Associations, and in 1892 meetings were held to celebrate this new union.

Probably the reason why this action did not feature in Northern Association affairs was that all the Baptist churches in the North East were already of the Particular Baptist tradition. This was in strong contrast to the situation in the Yorkshire Association where as a result of the union they saw their membership increase that year from ninety nine to 137 churches.

In 1885 the Wellington Street church in Stockton commenced the Northcote Street mission in the town which was later to become Lightfoot Grove Baptist Church and in 1888 it became an independent church with ninety nine members of the Wellington Street church becoming its founder members. Such a large number of founder members may be accounted for by the fact that this occurred the same time as the Wellington Street church withdrew from the Association, and these members perhaps wished to identify with a church which was in fellowship with the Association, because shortly after its formation the church applied for and was welcomed into membership of the Association. In 1893 the Association agreed to provide financial help to enable them to erect a new building, but it was not until 1904 that the church erected its new premises in Lightfoot Grove.

At the same time as establishing the Northcote Street mission, the Wellington Street church responded to an appeal for help from the Welsh Baptist Church in Portrack which was experiencing decline, and Portrack became a mission of the Wellington Street church. In 1907 the Welsh Baptist Association that owned the Portrack chapel gave the premises to the Wellington Street church and they maintained it for many years as a mission until 1980 when it became the independent Portrack Baptist Church.

A mission and Sunday School in Byker in Newcastle had been commenced in 1878 by the Tyneside churches, though the main responsibility for its work rested on the shoulders of the recently formed Jesmond Baptist Church, and its growth caused them to move in 1891 to larger premises in Denmark Street, in the Heaton area of the city. With the population of Byker/Heaton now reaching 50,000 the Association decided to give this work special help. In addition a substantial grant was received from the Baptist Union Church Extension Fund which had been set up after the Union's 1892 Assembly specifically to help in the erection of buildings in new areas.

All this help resulted in the mission becoming a constituted church in 1896, and two years later they opened their large new building in Heaton Road and became known as Heaton Baptist Church. By the year 1900 their membership was in excess of 200, and at that time they wrote a letter thanking the Association for their support and informing them that they were now in a position to meet all their obligations without the need of the Association's financial help. When the church moved to Heaton they continued holding Sunday services and running a Sunday School in the Byker area until the beginning of the war in 1914.

A few Baptist families who lived in Alnwick and who worshipped in various churches in the town contacted the Rev W J Packer, pastor of the Berwick Baptist Church, in 1883 about the possible formation of a Baptist church in Alnwick. In response to this approach David Ross, the town missionary in Berwick, conducted a mission in Alnwick, and as a result regular Sunday afternoon services began to be held in the Old Theatre, then standing empty. The following year it was decided to form a Baptist church, and David Ross accepted the members' invitation to serve as pastor. Two Presbyterian churches in the town amalgamated leaving their Lisburn Street premises unoccupied, and the Baptist church began meeting there in 1888. Initially they rented the building, but a few years later purchased it from the Presbyterians. About 1890 the church established a mission in Rosebrough, a small farming community nine miles north of Alnwick. In 1908 by mutual agreement the members who served there formed themselves into an independent, undenominational church, but due to movements in population this church closed a few years later.

Although the population of South West Durham in the latter part of the nineteenth century showed a large increase due to the opening up of the new coal mines, the six Baptist churches in that area (Wolsingham, Hamsterley, Crook, Witton Park, Bishop Auckland and Spennymoor) reported a considerable decline in membership, and it became evident that each church, with the exception of Crook, could no longer support their own full-time pastor. The Association appointed a deputation in 1895 to examine with the churches the possibility of grouping them together for pastoral oversight, but the deputation members reported back that the six churches did not favour the idea, and consequently the proposed scheme was not pursued. The Association, however, felt that some form of grouping was essential before they could justify giving financial support for ministry, and as a result of this decision some of the churches adopted a more limited linking scheme with two churches having a joint pastorate.

In 1896 the Grange Road church in Darlington considered establishing a mission in the north end of the town to serve a new and rapidly growing housing area in which some of their members lived. A corrugated iron hall seating 250 was erected in Corporation Road and services began to be held there in 1897. Regular missions were conducted in the area, and by 1902 the hall could barely accommodate those attending the services. In 1904 the Grange Road church consented to the request that the congregation at Corporation Road be established as an independent church, and the new church was constituted with thirty six founder members. The following year they appointed their own pastor and erected a new building at a cost of £4760. In the first two years of the new church's existence, sixty seven members were added to the church roll, and by 1910 membership was 150. During the first six years of the church's existence, five of their members responded to God's call to serve in overseas missionary work.

A situation which was to cause much distress and which eventually involved the Baptist Union secretary was the Association receiving in 1898 a letter from the Yorkshire Baptist Association informing them that the Wellington Street church in Stockton had applied to them to be admitted as a member church of their Association (the church had withdrawn from the Northern Baptist Association in 1889 following the 'Downgrade Controversy'). After long discussion the Association agreed that the following resolution be forwarded to the Yorkshire Association: "The committee of this Association

## Membership of churches affiliated
## to the Northern Association
## during the Nineteenth Century

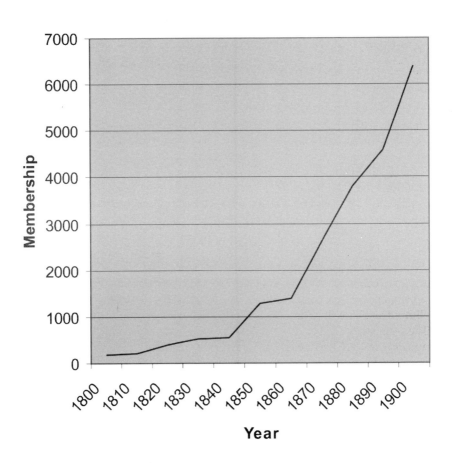

learns with sincere regret that the Yorkshire Association proposes to admit the church at Wellington Street, Stockton into its membership, and submits that no reason (theological or otherwise) exists to justify such departure from the recognised procedure of the Denomination, and respectfully submits to the consideration of the Committee of the Yorkshire Association whether the admission of the said church is under the circumstances justifiable. In the view of this committee if the Yorkshire Association receives this church it practically amounts to a vote of censure on the Northern Association."

The Association took two further steps. The committee agreed to send "a cordial invitation" to the Wellington Street church to rejoin the Association and assured them that in their communication with the Yorkshire Baptist Association they had no intention to do anything disrespectful or unbrotherly to the Stockton church. In addition they proposed that a sub-committee of both Associations meet at Stockton under the independent chairmanship of the minister of the Accrington Baptist Church in Lancashire to discuss the issue.

The Wellington Street church refused to alter their decision to join the Yorkshire Association, and the Yorkshire Association wrote to the Northern Association asking them to withdraw their protest. The Northern Association committee unanimously agreed to abide by their original decision since they could not find sufficient cause or reason for the church to take the proposed action. They also informed the Yorkshire Association that if they received the church into membership they would be creating a dangerous precedent.

By this time the Baptist Union was involved and the Rev J H Shakespeare, the new Union secretary, wrote to both Associations proposing that the situation be referred to arbitration, two of the four arbitrators being Dr John Clifford and himself. Sadly, even this proposal did not resolve the situation. The church did not become a member of the Yorkshire Association, and it was only in 1907 that the breach was finally healed and the church received back into the Northern Association. One welcome sign of this healing was the Association's acceptance of the church's invitation to host its Annual Assembly in 1909 in the new large premises seating 900 people which they had opened in 1903. On the opening of this new building the church decided to rename itself as Stockton Baptist Tabernacle.

Applications from churches seeking financial help continued to be received, and the amounts being requested far outweighed the resources of both the

Association and the Baptist Union Home Mission Fund. The Rev S H Booth, Baptist Union secretary, visited the North East in October 1896 and had a meeting which lasted four hours at which the representatives of each applying church were called in turn into the meeting and their particular situation discussed in detail. Mr Booth spoke of the problems being faced by the members of the Baptist Union Grants Committee, and being made aware of the national financial situation, several churches agreed to reduce the amount of the grant for which they were applying.

In 1897 Mr Booth wrote asking the Association's support for a 'Board of Introduction' which had been set up by the Baptist Union. Its purpose was to introduce ministers to churches that were seeking a pastor. Although the Association decided they could give 'no organised assistance to the Board', they agreed that they would recommend churches seeking ministers to communicate with the Board. This was the first step that eventually led under the secretaryship of the Rev J H Shakespeare to the appointment of Area Superintendents throughout the country, one of whose tasks was to facilitate the settlement of ministers in churches seeking pastors.

In 1898 after twenty one years service Mr Booth had to resign as Baptist Union secretary due to ill health, and the minutes of the Association record a glowing and lengthy tribute to his work and leadership. The Rev J H Shakespeare who succeeded him was to serve in that position for twenty six years, and under his secretaryship the Union (to which churches and Associations were looking increasingly for help) created new structures and erected an imposing new headquarters building in London which were to serve the denomination for most of the twentieth century.

Many churches used the imminent advent of the twentieth century as a springboard for further advance, and most of the Association churches identified with a "Forward Movement" and gave support to the Baptist Union's launch of a Twentieth Century Fund of £250,000 of which half was to be used for church extension in areas where no Baptist witness existed.

As the nineteenth century drew to a close, a spirit of optimism still pervaded the Association. For over twenty five years the Association had seen the largest growth in its history and it now had 43 churches with 6386 members and 9733 Sunday School scholars. The Association began explorations into the possible establishment of new Baptist centres of witness in Blyth, Shildon, Elswick, Whitley Bay and two new areas in Sunderland and Teesside.

# Chapter 12.

# First Signs of Decline 1900-1920

## An Industrial Heartland

As we begin looking at the life of the churches in the twentieth century, some may find it helpful to know something of the major changes that took place in the region. During the nineteenth century the North East had become a vast industrial heartland dominated by the three industries of coal mining, shipbuilding and steelmaking. By the end of the twentieth century these three main sources of employment had all but disappeared. A brief sketch of each industry reveals the extent of the changes.

In the seventeenth century around 400 ships operated from Newcastle carrying coal to London and other British towns. During the next 200 years the quantity of coal being mined from North East pits continued to increase until by the beginning of the twentieth century annual production was about fifty million tons – a quarter of total national production. Three new shipping ports – Seaham, Hartlepool and Middlesbrough – were built to handle the increasing trade.

The employment figures in the 1911 County Durham Census show that 281,291 males were in employment, and of these 132,005 (47%) worked in the coal mining industry. In 1991 the last of the pits in the county closed. To illustrate the impact of this change, it may be helpful to take as an example a typical coal mining town like Crook, ten miles south west of Durham City. The 1951 Census showed that in the area served by the Crook Employment Exchange there were 4700 people employed in coal mining. In the 1971 Census that figure was 150. Even with many moving elsewhere for work, including some taking advantage of a government sponsored emigration programme, many mining communities had over 50% unemployment, one even recording a rate of almost 90%.

In the 1830s Sunderland became the most important shipbuilding centre in the country, and by 1850 it had seventy six shipbuilding yards near the mouth of the River Wear producing about one third of all the ships built in the United Kingdom. Shortly after this, large shipbuilding yards were erected on the River Tyne, and on a smaller scale on the River Tees. During the Second World War 27% of the total tonnage of merchant shipping built in the United Kingdom came from Sunderland shipyards. Yet in 1988 the last of the town's shipyards closed down, and practically all the shipyards on the River Tyne shared the same fate.

With the discovery of iron ore deposits at Consett and at Eston near Middlesbrough, and because of a plentiful supply of good coking coal nearby, many ironworks sprang up throughout the region. By 1874 Middlesbrough was the biggest ironmaking town in England, producing one third of the nation's total output. From 1875 the ironworks changed to steel making following Sir Henry Bessemer's invention of the steel making process that bears his name, and production continued at high levels. Of the ten million tons of steel produced nationally in 1919 almost three and a half million tons came from nine steel plants in Middlesbrough. As the twentieth century proceeded most steel plants closed and production greatly diminished.

This decline in industrial production affected all levels of society. When unemployment in Jarrow reached 80% in 1936, 200 of the unemployed men there set out on the famous Jarrow March to London. Leaving the town on 5 October they walked 274 miles, arriving at Westminster on 31 October, challenging the government to take action to alleviate the poverty they and their families were experiencing. Things have greatly improved since then as a result of many new business initiatives, particularly in the service sector, but despite these improvements the unemployment rate has been and still is higher than the national rate.

**Reaching out to New Areas**

As the twentieth century dawned there was still a spirit of optimistic advance pervading the Association and many of the churches. In March 1900 the Association appointed a sub-committee who gave considerable time and effort to the establishing of a Baptist church in Whitley Bay. They commenced Sunday services and initially the average weekly attendance was 45. They decided on the erection of a chapel without delay, and within four months of beginning to hold services they purchased land in Oxford Street. The following year a chapel was built and opened for use. Also within four months of starting services, the Association agreed that they would give a grant of £70 towards the stipend of a minister on condition that the church contributed £50, and two months later the Rev F J H Humphrey, a student of Spurgeon's College, accepted the invitation to the pastorate of the church. Within three years the church had 100 members. In later years Mr Humphrey was awarded the D.S.O. for services as a chaplain to the forces during the 1914-1918 war, and in 1938 was elected President of the Baptist Union.

Consideration was also given at this time to developing work in the Benwell area in the west of Newcastle. When the Bewick Street church moved from its location in Newcastle city centre in 1886 and became two churches in Westgate Road and Jesmond, the Westgate Road congregation accepted responsibility for continuing to support a Sunday School in Tuthill Stairs. This work was later moved to Elswick Road in the west end of Newcastle, and in 1899 the church erected a hall and established a mission there in addition to the work of the Sunday School. The Rev W R Chesterton was appointed to oversee the development of this new work, and some indication of its rapid growth can be seen in the fact that the statistical figures of the Association in 1903 records the Benwell church as having 177 members. In 1904 it became known as Benwell Baptist Church.

In the first fourteen years of the twentieth century, six new Baptist churches were constituted. Mention has already been made of Whitley Bay, Benwell (Newcastle) and Corporation Road (Darlington). The other three were Wallsend, Oxford Road (Hartlepool) and Dean Bank (Ferryhill). The Dean Bank area of Ferryhill was growing rapidly due to the opening up of the large Dean and Chapter Colliery, and in 1903 the Spennymoor church began holding services there in rented premises. In 1906 the Spennymoor church agreed to contribute £100 towards the erection of a chapel, and the following year the Association contacted all the churches encouraging them to give financial support to the new cause. This resulted in the new Dean Bank chapel being opened in 1908, and the following year the members constituted themselves into an independent church. The Association agreed to a grant enabling the church to have a joint pastorate with Spennymoor, and this arrangement for pastoral oversight continued for many years.

Wallsend was growing rapidly as a major centre for shipbuilding, and in 1908 Mr W Galloway, a member of the Jarrow church, began holding services there in a room above a shop in High Street. By 1909 the congregation had grown significantly enough to encourage the members to constitute themselves as a church and consider erecting their own chapel. Initially they planned to buy a plot of land covering forty square yards for £170 and erecting an iron building costing £250. The Association, however, encouraged them to look for something larger and also expressed the view that an iron building was not desirable. The church acted on the Association's advice, abandoned the scheme and continued to meet in rented premises in North View, which they eventually purchased in 1919. Initially

91

the church was not able to support a pastor even with the help of a grant. In 1913 the Association asked the church to explore the possibility of a joint pastorate with either Heaton or North Shields. Neither of these options were pursued, and Mr John Raw was appointed lay pastor and under his leadership the church saw growth with average congregations of eighty.

The Tower Street church in Hartlepool, whose new building had been opened in 1890, saw significant growth during the twenty year ministry of the Rev Alfred Curwood. In his first ten years as pastor 231 members had been added to the church roll and the Sunday School had grown from eighty five to 300 scholars. This growth caused the church to renovate and add to their premises, and the building extensions were opened in 1901. Two years later Mr Curwood encouraged some of the church members to consider work beyond the Tower Street premises, and in 1903 the Cornwall Street Mission was opened in another part of the town. This extension work prospered which necessitated seeking larger premises. They erected a marquee for use in the summer months which could accommodate 230 people, and this was used for several years, and in 1906 they extended their accommodation in Cornwall Street by using the adjoining premises and making the necessary alterations to accommodate the growing congregations.

In 1909 the workers in Cornwall Street constituted themselves as a Baptist church with fifty four founding members, and in 1914 erected their own chapel in Oxford Road. Mr G J Bell, under whose leadership the Cornwall Street Mission was established, and Mr E Stephenson served the church as honorary pastors until 1926, after which the church was led by full-time ministers.

The Grainger family was a remarkable pioneering family and holds an honoured place in the growth of Baptist witness in Hartlepool. Captain Phatuel Grainger and his wife Mary were two of the founding members of the first Hartlepool church that was formed in 1845, and a few years later they were among the twelve members who established the new church in West Hartlepool in 1862 which erected its own chapel in Tower Street. In later years Mary Grainger's enthusiasm for extending Christ's Kingdom caused her to enlist the help of her children and grandchildren in establishing the third Hartlepool church in Oxford Road, seven members of the family being founder members. She lived long enough to lay a foundation stone of that church's new building in 1913. One of Mary's grandchildren, Theo Grainger (named after Theodosia Angus – a well-known Baptist family) was baptised in 1913 in the 'Joiner's Shop' in Cornwall Street. She died in 1997 having been a member of the Oxford Road church for eighty four years, and during her long life she contributed significantly to Christian witness both in Hartlepool and further afield.

In 1903 several of the members of the Jarrow church under the leadership of Mr Hugh Adam formed the church that became known as the 'Welcome Baptists'. Initially they met in premises in South Street, but there are no records of their ongoing work which would suggest that the work was perhaps disbanded after several years.

The congregation at Shotley Field in Derwentside had declined to such an extent that in 1903 the chapel was let to the Methodists and finally sold to them in 1910. It is probable that the few remaining members identified with the nearby Highgate church which at that time was flourishing with a membership of around 175 and a Sunday School of almost 250 scholars. The cramped nature of the site at Highgate did not allow any extension of their premises, so the church purchased a plot of land in 1905 with a view to erecting a larger building. It was some years before they got down to serious plans, but the advent of the war in 1914 caused further postponement. The plot of land they had purchased was sold in favour of a new location in Blackhill, a built up area on the northern outskirts of Consett, and their new building was opened in 1925, and thereafter the church was known as Blackhill Baptist Church. During the first two years of meeting in the new building, membership of the church increased from 136 to 161.

Another church in that area was to experience change. The village of Broomley in the Tyne Valley had become depopulated and in 1905 the members of the church that met there decided to relocate their place of meeting to Stocksfield, a village two miles away which was developing into a commuter area for the affluent middle class who worked in Newcastle. The stones of the old Broomley chapel were used in the erection of the new building, and when opened the church was renamed Stocksfield Baptist Church. The church continued the arrangement of a joint pastorate with the Broomhaugh church.

Although new churches were being established at this time, it is worth noting that several other initiatives that were undertaken then did not result in the establishment of a permanent work. Attempts to begin a new work at Shildon met with some initial success. Mr A R Doggart of the Bishop Auckland church purchased the disused Friends' Meeting House in the town and under the honorary pastoral oversight of Major Andrew McGill, also of Bishop Auckland, it was opened as a Baptist mission. However, after several years the cause languished and services were discontinued in 1910. Four

Baptist families lived in Willington, and the Association asked the Spennymoor church if their minister could devote one day a week to work with these families with a view to the possible establishing of a church. Although meetings began to be held, very little progress was made partly due to the fact that the owner of the main coal mine in the town was a devoted, almost obsessive, Methodist New Connexion churchman. His considerable influence in the community prevented other Free Church denominations, including the other Methodist denominations, from gaining a strong foothold in the town. It would seem that the Baptist families in Willington identified with Baptist churches in neighbouring towns, and the prospect of a local Baptist witness faded away.

For several years a mission had existed in Langley Moor, a village three miles south west of the city of Durham, largely under the auspices of the Witton Park church, but in 1908 that church informed the Association that they could no longer maintain the work there. The Association approached the Waterhouses Group of Churches, indicating that if their lay preachers would maintain the services the Association would pay all travelling expenses. The Waterhouses Group responded positively and accepted responsibility for the preaching ministry. In 1920 difficulties arose concerning the premises in Langley Moor and since they had not been resolved by 1926 the building was sold and shortly after this meetings ceased to be held.

An Extension and Evangelisation Committee was formed by the Association in 1908 with a specific remit to explore how Baptist witness could be extended in the North East. The first two towns suggested by the committee as possible locations for new causes were Blyth and Chester-le-Street. There is no record of any work ever being done in Chester-le-Street at this time, but in 1910 the Association Committee asked the Extension Committee to start a work in Blyth, then a town of over 30,000 people, by adopting the lines taken a few years earlier in the successful establishing of the work in Whitley Bay. Services began to be held in June of that year, and within a year the committee reported that the work was 'exceedingly promising', and recommended that the Association purchase for £800 a site in Croft Road with a view to building a chapel. The initial promising outlook did not continue and by 1913 the committee reported that the work was not progressing as they had expected and had 'practically collapsed'. Shortly afterwards the Association decided to terminate the tenancy of the premises they were using, and services were discontinued.

When the Rev E A Carter of an evangelistic organisation known as the Pioneer Mission heard this news, he approached the Association and offered to place a missioner in Blyth if they would give an annual grant of £30 towards his salary. The Association agreed to this request and services were re-commenced in 1914. Unfortunately the following year the missioner had to withdraw from the work at short notice due to health reasons and the Pioneer Mission appointed a new missioner who reported an average attendance of 40 at the Sunday services. Services continued to be held for several years, but the 1920 report to the Association stated that 'progress of any kind is impossible in the present building'. That year Mr Harry Baxendale, a former missionary in India, expressed a willingness to lead the work in Blyth, and the Association agreed to contribute towards his stipend. The congregation vacated their unsatisfactory premises and decided to maintain a Sunday School work in one of the Council Schools, but things did not work out as planned, and in December 1920 the Association reluctantly decided to terminate all work in Blyth. Although the extant records do not give specific reasons for the changing fortunes that were experienced at Blyth, some indications would suggest that one main factor was the non-emergence of any local leadership during the ten years that were spent trying to establish a permanent work.

**Ups and downs of existing churches**

In 1902 concern was raised about the future of the church at Brough. A small committee was appointed by the Association to meet with the church and discuss the situation, and the committee felt that realistic help should be looked for mainly from the other four churches in the Westmorland Group. This raised the whole issue of the Group's relationship with the Association, for in 1905 the five churches in the Group, which all had relatively small memberships due to their rural locations, wrote to the Association expressing a feeling of isolation from the other churches in the Association. To go a small way towards meeting this need, it was agreed that each year a representative from the Association would spend at least one week in the Westmorland area ministering to the churches and its members. In addition the Association agreed in 1907 to support the appointment of a well-paid pastor, due to the expense of travel between the churches, and two years later they decided to give a further grant to enable the churches to appoint an assistant pastor. The financial burden this imposed on the churches proved to be too great, and the arrangement was short lived. By 1913 most of the members of the Brough church had moved from the area and shortly afterwards the church was closed and the building sold.

In 1918 it was proposed that the Westmorland Group of Churches establish links with the Westmorland Congregational churches for pastoral oversight. Representatives from both groups were appointed to see whether this was feasible, and if so to prepare an outline scheme of union, but within one year the scheme was abandoned, due to (as the minutes record) 'local difficulties'.

A church which saw considerable growth at the beginning of the twentieth century was Durham Road, Gateshead. The Rev B Grey Griffiths, a student from Regents Park College, had his first pastorate at Durham Road from 1903 to 1908, and under his ministry the membership of the church grew to 379 and it became one of the leading centres of evangelical witness on Tyneside. In later years Mr Griffiths was appointed secretary of the Baptist Missionary Society, a post he held for many years.

Also at the beginning of the century several existing churches were involved in building works. The Spennymoor church completed the erection of new Sunday School premises and alterations to their chapel. The Wolsingham church purchased property adjacent to their chapel to provide accommodation for their growing Sunday School work. The Northcote Street church in Stockton purchased land in Lightfoot Grove and opened their new premises in 1904. The Rye Hill church in Newcastle sold their premises and used the proceeds to build new premises in Elswick Road, and the members renamed their church Wyclif Baptist Church. The South Bank church purchased a site for their new chapel.

Concern about the pastoral oversight of the eight churches in South West Durham was a regular item on the agenda of the Association Committee at this time (in fact, this was to continue for over sixty years!). None of the churches were large enough to support their own pastor, so the only way they could qualify for a pastoral grant was by linking with other churches. This, however, proved not to be an easy task for several reasons. In 1910 the eight churches (Hamsterley, Wolsingham, Bishop Auckland, Crook, Witton Park, Shildon, Spennymoor and Dean Bank) were asked to consider a grouping scheme for pastoral oversight, and the Association pledged itself to give favourable consideration to any financial arrangements should the eight churches reach agreement. Unfortunately, agreement could not be reached, so the Association proposed several joint pastorates with one minister responsible for two churches.

Even this proposal was not without its problems. For example, Hamsterley agreed to a joint pastorate with Wolsingham on condition that the minister resided at Hamsterley. Neither the Association or the Wolsingham church were happy about this condition, but Hamsterley was not prepared to alter its position. A pastor did undertake the joint pastorate in 1911, but by 1913 relationships between the two churches had deteriorated to such an extent that the Association advised the minister to seek another pastorate so that they could review the arrangement. Crook and Witton Park were linked, as were Spennymoor and Dean Bank, but in subsequent years different arrangements were frequently entered into, depending on the circumstances of each church. Unfortunately, personal differences between individuals sometimes created tensions and on at least one occasion the Association had to step in to try and bring about reconciliation.

In some of the Association minutes one detects an element of frustration and uncertainty about how best to help these churches. One factor that could have had a bearing on this situation was that the churches were located in small towns and villages within the Auckland coalfield. The whole area was beginning to experience a decline in population because the hey-day of coal mining in the area had passed. Aggressive competition from the continent, particularly Poland, was making it difficult for some of the mine owners finding a market for their coal. Lay offs, lock-outs and wage reductions on the part of the owners were matched by strikes on the part of the miners. Pits were being closed and no new ones were opened and this resulted in people, including church members, leaving the area for work elsewhere. This uncertainty about the future seems to have been reflected in the churches.

At the beginning of the twentieth century there were three Baptist churches in Middlesbrough. The Newport Road and Marton Road churches were members of the Northern Association and the Linthorpe Road church was in membership with the Yorkshire Association. In 1916 the Association appointed a sub-committee to discuss the future since these three churches were suggesting that they merge and form one strong Baptist church in the town, and since the Yorkshire Association had considerably greater financial resources than the Northern Association, it was being proposed that the new united church become a member of the Yorkshire Association. As a first step towards this union the Newport Road and Marton Road churches united in 1917, and the new church with a joint membership of 243 transferred its membership to the Yorkshire Association. The Linthorpe Road church joined the united church in 1919. Geographically these churches were in the county of Yorkshire, so the change did not cause any tensions between the two Associations, and the churches both north and south of the River Tees continued to maintain and foster good relationships with one another.

## Developments in the Association

With the continuing growth of the churches as the twentieth century dawned, the suggestion was made that the Northern Association may wish to follow the practice of other Associations in England by dividing itself into Districts (for example, the Yorkshire Association had divided itself into eight Districts). The main purpose of such an arrangement was that although the Association would still be the body with overall responsibility for the wellbeing of the churches, smaller groupings would enable more meaningful inter-church fellowship and the giving of active support among the churches. Many felt this would be advantageous in the Association, since the area it covered stretched about 100 miles from Berwick in the north to Middlesbrough in the south.

Some members of the Association committee were asked to draw up a scheme and if it was agreeable it would be implemented. The main area on which agreement was considered essential was in establishing what matters should be decided by the Districts and what should be decided by the Association Committee. In 1903 the Northern and Southern Divisions of the Association were created and officers duly appointed to serve both bodies. At this time the Northern District had 18 churches, and the Southern District 23 churches. The main matters dealt with by the District Committees were:

a) arranging twice-yearly united meetings (normally on a Wednesday afternoon and evening with guest speakers) and occasionally conferences on specific issues;

b) arranging an annual pulpit exchange and an annual Association visit to every church;

c) sharing news about the churches and suggesting or providing possible help where this was needed;

d) arranging for missionary speakers from the BMS to visit churches and also united missionary meetings; appointing visitors to grant-aided churches.

This arrangement of having two Districts continued until 1968 when, at the suggestion of the District Committees, it was agreed to abolish them. That year a new constitution was adopted making the Association the one body which dealt with all matters relating to the churches.

In view of the erection or enlargement of many church premises at this time, the Association committee felt the time had come to establish an Association Building Fund. Prior to this, whenever any church approached the

Association for financial help in meeting building costs, the only course open to the Association was to agree its approval of the scheme, commend it to the churches and invite them to send contributions to the particular church that was seeking help. Six years were to elapse before a Building Fund was eventually set up in 1910, the initial aim being to raise £7,000 through personal and church donations. The resources of this fund were able to meet only a small proportion of the amounts being asked for, and it operated by giving loans to help churches with their building projects. Some indication of the need for this kind of funding may be gauged by the fact that in 1904 the Association sent applications to the Baptist Union Twentieth Century Fund from nine churches which were seeking help with their building costs. In the following five years new building projects were undertaken by a further four churches.

A proposal was made in 1903 to form an organisation for lay preachers, and in 1906 the Lay Preachers' Federation was created, Major Andrew McGill of Bishop Auckland serving as its first secretary. This soon became a body which exercised a significant and positive influence on Association affairs, and by 1908 it had 134 members. One illustration of its influence is in the year following its formation it requested the Association to appoint an evangelist and promised an annual contribution of £50 towards his stipend. The Association agreed to this request but an appointment was not made because at the same time as they were taking steps towards an appointment the Association received a letter from Rev J H Shakespeare informing them that the Rev A W Evans had been appointed as a Baptist Union Evangelist, and Mr Shakespeare was keen that some of his work should be done in the North East. Over the next few years Mr Evans conducted missions in quite a number of the Association churches, and his ministry was warmly received.

The Baptist Union's 'Board of Introduction' which had been created in 1887 to assist churches seeking pastors and pastors seeking churches was now becoming the recognised way in which pastoral settlements were made throughout the land. In 1903 the Association agreed as a matter of policy that it would pass on all information about ministers and churches seeking changes to the Union to be dealt with by the Board of Introduction. The centralisation of this work placed considerable demands on the Union which they could not always meet satisfactorily. Having agreed beforehand the principle of full co-operation between the Union and the Associations in the matter of ministerial settlement, in 1915 the Baptist Union introduced the Ministerial Settlement and Sustentation Scheme. The major feature of the innovation was the division of the country into nine areas and the Baptist

Union appointing a full-time General Superintendent for each area. The North Eastern Area served both the Yorkshire and Northern Associations with the Superintendent residing in Leeds. An area committee to serve under the Superintendent was appointed, ten members being from Yorkshire and four from the Northern Association. In 1918 the Association sent a congratulatory letter to the Baptist Union on the success of ministerial settlement under the new scheme, since during its first year of operation it had overseen nationally the successful settlement of seventy six of the eighty ministers who had desired a change of pastorate.

The first North East Area Superintendent, the Rev J G Williams, took up his position in 1915, but unfortunately he had to take early retirement on health grounds in 1922. The Association used this as an opportunity to inform the Baptist Union that in their view it was not satisfactory that someone resident in Leeds should have oversight of the churches of the Northern Association. In their letter they said, "we earnestly urge before making a new appointment the Baptist Union consider the need to divide the area". Despite this appeal the Union appointed the Rev Henry Bonser as the new Area Superintendent, and the Association decided to take no further steps about the division of the area since they had received assurances from Mr Bonser that he would devote his energies to all the needs of the area.

It would seem that this issue of dividing the area had been raised earlier, since in 1920 the Union secretary, J H Shakespeare, had written to the Association saying that the Union would not create the Northern Association as a separate area. However, in his letter he asked the Association to consider the advisability of them appointing a full-time secretary to help the Superintendent in his work. The Association felt they could make such an appointment only if they had the full support of the churches, since such a step would require a considerable increase in contributions from the churches to the Association. Seventeen of the Association churches favoured the idea, but since there was a significant number that did not favour the proposal, the Association felt it could not proceed with such an appointment. However, they did agree to the proposal that a pastor of one of the smaller churches could be appointed who would divide his time between the Association and his church, with the Association paying an annual honorarium of £50.

At the 1902 Association Assembly the delegates agreed a resolution expressing strong opposition to a section of the Education Bill currently before Parliament. The major reform would see local authorities taking over responsibility for all primary and secondary schools, but the section to which exception was taken was that taxes and rates would finance Anglican and Catholic schools, yet these churches would still retain considerable freedom from local authority control. Opposition to this legislation was strongly expressed by nonconformist leaders and churches throughout the country. The Association continued to express its opposition over a number of years, including urging the Rev J H Shakespeare to send a deputation to the Prime Minister to express their concerns, and also writing to over 200 MPs who were sympathetic to the nonconformist position.

It is interesting to see the composition of the Association Committee around this time. For example, in 1915 it had thirty two members, thirteen being ministers and nineteen being laymen. Seven of the laymen were Justices of the Peace and at least four were either Aldermen or Town Councillors. One commendable feature is that several of these lay committee members displayed a special concern for the smaller churches and sought to encourage them by regular visits and also giving financial help. Up till 1918 the committee had been composed only of men, but in 1918 they agreed to the election of four women members. This arrangement remained unchanged until 1959 when the practice of having a separate vote for women members was discontinued.

During the last quarter of the nineteenth century the membership of Association Churches increased by over 40%, and this growth reached its peak in 1908, when 6458 members were reported. When the Newcastle and Gateshead Baptist Council was formed in 1902, the member churches of that Council reported having ten Sunday Schools, 2429 scholars and 231 teachers. It was around 1911 that statements began to appear indicating a change of mood regarding church life. In that year the Association acknowledged that the significant growth seen in the previous thirty five years was unlikely to continue at the same rate, in fact, only three new churches were planted during the next forty years in contrast to fifteen being planted in the previous forty years. Concern was expressed at the decline in the numbers of members and Sunday School scholars. Also in 1911 the Association circulated a document to the churches to encourage them in their work 'fully recognising the peculiar difficulties of all the Christian work at the present time'.

On the recommendation of the ministers' fraternal the Association ran a week long residential Summer Mission School at Whitley Bay in August 1912 with a special focus on training in evangelism. This event proved to be a great success with the numbers attending exceeding the expectations of the organisers. Some of the tutors were well-known national Baptist leaders.

When the venture was repeated the following year, numbers were even greater. The decision was made to make this an annual event, but unfortunately the outbreak of war prevented this from taking place in subsequent years and the practice was not revived until 1925.

## The First World War

Inevitably, war-time conditions greatly affected all the churches, and for most the emphasis was simply on maintaining their work. To give a picture of how the war affected Baptists in the North East, the following are examples from a few of the churches.

On 14 December 1914 the town of Hartlepool was bombarded by the German navy. The Baptist Church received a direct hit and as a result the building had to be demolished. 121 of the town's inhabitants were killed in the attack, including the Sunday School secretary and seven Sunday School children. The members promptly decided they would build a new church when the opportune time came, but services continued to be held due to the kindness of the local Wesleyan Church who offered them the use of their halls. This arrangement lasted until 1917 when the church transferred its meeting place to one of the rooms in the Town Hall. A new chapel was built in Regent Street and opened for use in 1921.

Several church premises were commandeered by the army. The Wolsingham schoolroom was taken over and used as a medical centre to care for soldiers who had been wounded in battle. Other churches had part of their premises used for a variety of purposes. In 1914 many Belgian families had to flee their country due to the German invasion, and came to Britain. The Grange Road, Darlington church agreed to rent a house in the town and accept responsibility for the support of two of these families for the duration of the war.

One hundred and forty young men connected with the three congregations of the Waterhouses Group served in the armed forces and twenty four of them were killed in action. Sixty of the members of the Corporation Road, Darlington church served in the forces of whom seventeen had been Sunday School teachers prior to their enlistment. Sixty seven members of the Grange Road, Darlington church joined the forces and seven of them were killed in action. Nearly every church experienced losses of life and many saw some of their young men return with permanent injuries. Although exact figures cannot be ascertained, the available information would suggest that between three hundred and four hundred men from Association churches were killed in the war. In 1919 the Association held a Memorial and Thanksgiving Service for the conclusion of the war at which the speaker was Lt Col A McGill, a member of the Bishop Auckland church. Prior to this, he had been very active in Association affairs, serving on the Association Committee for many years. He wrote the 1903 Association letter entitled "Non Attendance at Church", and served as moderator in 1905.

When the war ended in 1918 the Association affirmed that it was 'an excellent opportunity to advance', and in 1919 they approached all the churches with a proposal about how they 'could bring about the revival of church life throughout the Association'. As a first step they said there would be value in every church having an internal mission and they gave suggested guidelines that churches could follow should they undertake such an exercise. Two main stated objects of such a mission were: (1) "to teach the New Testament conception of the church and to deepen the consciousness of the meaning and responsibilities of church membership", and (2) "to consider the efficiency of the means employed for bringing young people to Christ". Over the next few years the Association gave help and guidance to encourage churches as they faced the new challenges of the post-war situation.

Although all churches had been affected by the war, many of the larger churches were still flourishing. For example, Stockton Tabernacle was recognised by many as the leading Free Church in that town. In the post-war years they arranged periodic public meetings to which members of all denominations were invited. They engaged well-known Christian leaders to speak at these meetings, among whom were Handley Moule and Hensley Henson, both Bishops of Durham. However, as the post-war years developed many of the Association churches saw a decline in membership. Many recognised that the days of growth were at an end and they would do well to maintain their church life at its existing level. Clearly the days ahead were full of uncertainty and challenge.

# Chapter 13.

# Much Labour, yet Little Fruit
# 1920-1945

In the 1920s there were frequent references to "the difficulties facing the churches in the post-war situation", and these difficulties were to continue for many years. The Association's Annual Report for 1930 states, "there is a feeling that the ordinary man in the street no longer sees anything attractive in the church, and therefore is indifferent to its appeals". Yet despite this bleak assessment, many of the churches placed an emphasis on evangelistic endeavour and there was also a widespread desire to expand Baptist witness in many areas where no Baptist church existed.

During the period under review in this chapter, five main concerns were regularly addressed by the churches and the Association in the light of this new situation. These were:

a)     concern about the spiritual state of the churches resulting in a call to commitment and the need for a new emphasis on spirituality and evangelism;

b)     the continuing and in some cases rapid decline in Sunday School and Youth Work, and the need for some kind of bold action to try and reverse this trend;

c)     the need to provide help to the smaller country churches, most of which were in communities with a decreasing population due to the adverse economic conditions;

d)     the pressing financial needs felt by many churches, and the need for greater giving to Association and Union funds to meet the increasing number of requests for financial help;

e)     the desire to plant churches in areas where there was no Baptist witness.

In 1928 it was reported to the Association Committee that a new Baptist church had been formed in Redcar with thirty one founder members and that prospects for growth seemed bright. The church became a member of the Yorkshire Association. In 1930 the church at Thornaby was planning to erect a building in a new part of the town, and they sought financial help from the Yorkshire Association, but were informed by them that their rules restricted the giving of grants to member churches. Following a meeting with representatives of the Yorkshire and Northern Associations, it was agreed that the church transfer its membership to Yorkshire. The new building in Thorntree Road was opened in 1933. The church decided to continue the holding of services in both of their buildings for a few years, but in 1937 all the work that centred on their old building in Westbury Street was transferred to their new premises, and the old building was sold.

In 1931 the South Bank church followed the action taken by the Thornaby church the previous year and also joined the Yorkshire Association. This meant that all the Cleveland Baptist churches south of the River Tees were now in membership with the Yorkshire Association. That same year, however, a Cleveland Group of Churches was formed uniting all the churches on Teesside whether belonging to the Northern or Yorkshire Associations, and regular fellowship was maintained between them in subsequent years.

In 1925 the Association set up a Commission of Enquiry because of growing concern about the decline in the numbers of children and young people in the churches. In their report they adjudged that the key problem was the lack of leadership and competent teachers, yet they did not paint a wholly pessimistic picture. At this time both Districts of the Association began a youth ministry with two successful and well supported youth conferences being held in 1928. This joint work continued to grow and Youth Councils were appointed and made responsible for organising events. Weekend youth conferences and other youth meetings were held each year, and these events were widely supported by almost every church. Some of these events had a specific form such as training in reaching other young people for Christ, and the challenge of world mission. In addition, the Youth Councils arranged for teams of young people who led Sunday services in some of our churches. This development in youth work was one of the most encouraging features between the two wars.

From 1932 onwards most Association churches became involved in Discipleship Campaigns, many of them being led by ministers within the Association. Materials were produced outlining a suggested programme, and guidance was given on their conduct. The Campaign covered many areas of church life, among which were prayer, personal witness, how to lead people to faith in Christ, work among young people, making contact with parents of Sunday School children, lay preaching and arranging guest services. The holding of these Campaigns continued for three years, and while they brought undoubted benefit to the churches and resulted in many new evangelistic initiatives, they did not result in any great influx of new members into the churches. The moderator of the 1935 Assembly, Mr H W Robinson of South Shields, devoted his address to a review of the Discipleship Campaigns held over the previous three years, and acknowledged that the results fell far short of expectations. That year only seventy five baptisms took place in all the Association churches. The minutes of that Assembly stated that not only were many of the Sunday Schools a shadow of their former selves, but that very few Sunday School scholars were going on to church membership.

## Planting new churches

In 1923 the Association appointed a committee to examine the possibilities of Baptist witness being established in Ashington, Chester-le-Street and Shilbottle. Although exploratory work was done, no permanent work was established in any of these locations. It would seem that planting a Baptist church in a new location was likely to make progress only if there were some Baptists already living in that place who were prepared to commit themselves to that work. A good example of this is seen in the formation of the church at Easington Colliery.

In 1926 (as a consequence of the General Strike of that year) several Baptist families moved from Waterhouses to Easington Colliery to work in the new mines being opened in that area, and they were keen to begin a Baptist witness in their new community. They commenced holding services in November 1926 in the local Council School, and initial reports described the work as 'very successful'. By July 1927 twelve members had constituted themselves as a church, and they began seeking a site for building a chapel. As an encouragement to this new cause, the Association agreed that the proceeds from the sale of the recently closed Langley Moor building be devoted to the Easington Colliery building fund. The Association suggested that the church at West Hartlepool be approached to see if they would provide pastoral leadership, but this was not pursued since the Waterhouses church had indicated a wish to provide this. In 1929 the church opened their new building, and in 1933 by arrangement with the Waterhouses church they appointed their own lay pastor who worked under the guidance of the minister at West Hartlepool.

During the 1920s several people had been holding services in the Grangetown area of Teesside, and in 1930 they decided to erect their own building. Some of the members of the South Bank church helped them in this work and it became well established. For many years it operated as a mission, and in 1960 was established as a Baptist church.

In 1930 a new work was emerging in Billingham, largely due to the efforts of lay preachers from West Hartlepool and Stockton. Shortly after commencing services the lay preachers asked for help from the Association in securing a site for building a Baptist Church, but they were unable to assist since the Association had no funds for building purchases. Due to certain difficulties the work was discontinued in 1932, but some of the young men who were involved had hopes for Baptist witness in the town.

The next record we have is of eleven residents in Billingham, most of whom were members of neighbouring Baptist churches, meeting together on January 1942 with a view to establishing a Baptist church. They began holding services and prayer meetings. By the following year their membership had increased to twenty two, a temporary building was opened for their meetings, and Mr Henry Bond, moderator and treasurer of the Association, accepted the church's invitation to be their honorary pastor. On retiring from business in 1946 Mr Bond devoted himself full-time to the leadership of the church and continued in this until his death in 1950, by which time the membership had reached fifty. In 1946 a site was purchased and in 1950 the new church building was opened, and in recognition of Mr Bond's major contribution to the growth of the church, it was named the Henry S Bond Memorial Hall.

When the Rev Ernest Godfrey became minister of the church in Grange Road, Darlington, in 1926 he established a Thursday night 'Men's Class', and four of these men met with the Grange Road deacons in 1930 and informed them that twenty men in the class were looking for a place in the town where they could do pioneer work, and they suggested the Geneva Road area as a possible location. Mr Arthur Doggart, one of the deacons, said he was willing to pay for a site if the church agreed to the plan. In the event, he contributed over 50% of the cost of the building that was eventually erected. A Sunday evening service and a Sunday School were commenced in 1930, and in 1932 a commodious school and chapel was opened and sufficient adjoining land purchased to enable future extension of the premises. The work prospered and operated as a mission of the Grange Road church until 1947, when forty three members transferred their membership from the mother church to become founder members of the newly constituted Geneva Road Baptist Church.

# Mixed fortunes

As the twentieth century progressed the Ford Forge church in north Northumberland which had been formed in 1806 experienced a decline in attendance. The area was sparsely populated, and the church report for 1920 said that most of its members were elderly and were finding transport difficult because they did not live in the immediate vicinity. As a result the members closed the church in 1922 and most of them transferred to the Baptist church in Berwick, eight miles way.

An ongoing experience of some of the smaller churches was the difficulty in making pastoral settlements. In 1922 the Association felt that the growing work at Wallsend needed full-time pastoral oversight and they pledged their help to make this possible. Over a period of two years the church issued an invitation to the pastorate to several ministers but they all declined. Faced with this ongoing disappointment the church approached the Jarrow church for help, and the two churches agreed unanimously to have a joint pastorate. Several ferry crossings which operated frequently on the River Tyne meant that travel between Jarrow and Wallsend was not difficult. Not only did some of the other smaller churches find difficulty securing pastors, but very few of those pastors stayed any longer than three or four years.

In 1929 the Baptist Union appointed the Rev Robert Snaith as an evangelist to serve the Northern Association. The initial arrangement was that he would devote six months to the church at Wallsend and six months to evangelistic work among the churches. Mr Snaith served in this way for four years and each year he led on average six church-based evangelistic campaigns throughout the North East. When his period of service was ended he was thanked for his excellent service to the churches which in most cases had met with considerable success.

Although overall the picture at this time was one of decline, there were many bright spots on the church scene, one such being at South Bank near Middlesbrough. In 1929 the Rev Alfred Queen, a young bachelor, had ended a ministry in London and was planning to emigrate to Canada. In the few weeks prior to him sailing, he accepted an invitation to minister at the South Bank church. Amazing results followed his preaching of the gospel, and the church unanimously pressed him to consider a call to the pastorate. He felt led to forego moving to Canada, cancelled his sailing, and accepted the church's invitation. In his first year there were fifty four baptisms of new believers, most of whom were between the ages of eighteen and thirty. Although he stayed for just over three years at the church, many young people responded to his ministry, and an average of four hundred people attended the Sunday evening services at which he preached.

Another encouraging situation was at Jarrow. In 1932 over forty young people took to the streets of the town after the six o'clock Sunday service and invited people to a service at eight o'clock which was especially geared to non-churchgoers. On some occasions there were over six hundred people at these services and many came to faith in Christ. A few years later in 1938 an additional outreach of the Jarrow church was the beginning of a Sunday School in the Monkton district of the town.

Several of the Association churches undertook building projects in the years between the two world wars. The opening of the new Blackhill church in 1925 has already been mentioned. That same year the Ushaw Moor church opened their new school building – the John Raw Memorial School. The congregation formed in Middlesbrough as a result of the union of the three churches in the town opened their new premises in Southfield Road in 1928. In 1929 the Lightfoot Grove church in Stockton erected a new hall on a site adjoining their existing building. The Whitley Bay church opened their new building in 1931. The following year the Oxford Road church in Hartlepool purchased land adjoining their existing premises, and in 1937 drew up plans for a new church and schoolroom. The South Bank church opened their new schoolroom in 1934. In 1937 the three Baptist churches in South Shields worked together to establish a new church in the Cleadon Park/Harton area of the town. They obtained a site but the advent of the war in 1939 halted their plans to erect a church. It was 1957 before their extension plans were fulfilled with the opening of a new building in Marsden Road. A similar postponement due to the war was experienced by the Wallsend church. In 1939 they secured a site on the new Battle Hill housing estate, but building work did not proceed until a few years after the conclusion of the war.

In 1924 the Baptist Missionary Society made it known that it needed to increase its annual income by at least £50,000 to meet its growing work. The Rev John McBeath visited the North East on behalf of the BMS and spoke at the Association and church meetings to encourage greater giving. The Association agreed to support this appeal and commended it to all the churches, and they specifically appealed to ministers, believing that their strong advocacy was the key to success. Although giving was increased it was never adequate enough, and by 1931 the BMS was informing the churches that it could no longer meet the needs of all its mission stations due to lack of finance.

Financial pressures from several directions were being felt at this time. The churches in the declining coal mining communities were particularly affected as a result of unemployment, causing many of their members to emigrate or move elsewhere in the country for work. Some of these churches reported that unemployment in their area was above 50%. Two or three of these churches had incurred debts which they were unable to pay off, and to avert trouble the Association had to meet these bills.

In 1925 thirteen churches applied for grants to enable them to pay the stipends of their ministers, but the amounts requested far exceeded what was available. The following year to try and formulate some kind of financial policy the Association sent a questionnaire to all the churches regarding their giving. All but three of the churches responded, and in the light of their replies they prepared a document. Copies of this were circulated to the churches, and it was agreed that finance would be the main subject to be considered at the 1927 Annual Assembly. One of the conclusions they reached was that if ministry was going to be provided for all the churches in the Association, the further grouping of churches was necessary, and even the adoption of a circuit pattern of ministry.

An additional pressure at this time was the appeal for £300,000 for the Baptist Union Superannuation Scheme, and considering all the other pressing claims, it is remarkable that in 1927 the Association churches raised £7,500 in response to this appeal.

An additional appeal for money was made in 1936 when the Baptist Union launched a Forward Movement at a meeting in the Royal Albert Hall in London. Its twofold purpose was evangelistic and financial. A national appeal for £1,000,000 was launched and this amount was reached in 1941. The money was to be used for evangelistic work and church planting. One church that benefited from this scheme was Benwell in the west end of Newcastle, a grant from the fund enabling them to erect a new building in 1937.

## Dedicated laypeople

For many years the churches had been blessed by laymen of a high spiritual calibre such as Henry Bond who contributed so much to the life of the churches. Space prevents mention of most of them, but it may be worthy to take note of three men who died in 1931/32 whose contributions were outstanding. Alderman G W Bartlett, J.P. had been a deacon of the Grange Road church in Darlington for sixty years, and for fifty years had held several offices within the Association. In 1893 he became the first Baptist Mayor of Darlington. He was widely respected for his public service throughout County Durham and for many years was the Chief Magistrate of Darlington.

Mr Irving A Hodgson spent his early life in Hamsterley, but moved to Newcastle in 1898 and was a very active member of the Jesmond church for thirty three years. He was noted for his passion for evangelism, playing a prominent role in establishing and maintaining the work at Whitley Bay and Wallsend. When the latter church eventually opened its new building on the Battle Hill estate, it recognised his outstanding contribution by naming themselves the Irving A Hodgson Memorial Church.

As a young man Mr Arthur Doggart moved from Glasgow to Bishop Auckland and worked in a small store in the town, becoming its manager and eventually its owner. Using his store as a base he built a large clothing and furniture business with twelve departmental stores in towns throughout County Durham. He moved to Darlington and joined the Grange Road church. He devoted a significant proportion of the profits of his business to Christian work. A substantial gift from him enabled the Association to establish the Church Extension Fund. He was an enthusiast for church planting and gave freely to new projects, two of which were the new Thornaby church and the new cause in Geneva Road, Darlington which had been started by men from his home church. He also proved to be a good ambassador for the North East on the national Baptist scene. In 1921 he was appointed chairman of the BMS General Committee and in 1928 was elected President of the Baptist Union.

**The Second World War**

The Second World War years were marked by the churches making every effort to maintain their witness. The blackout restrictions caused some churches to change the times of their services and make alterations to their church programmes. The military took over part of the premises of many of the churches, and this caused restrictions in their activities. For example, they took over the entire premises at Dean Bank, Ferryhill, with the exception of the vestry, and all the church's Sunday services and activities were limited to what was possible within that one room. Six of the Association churches were damaged by enemy action, but the churches of Whitley Bay and Lindsey Road, Sunderland were the only two churches where damage was so extensive as to prevent the use of the sanctuary for Sunday worship.

During the later years of the war much discussion focussed on the issues that would be faced by the churches in the post-war years. The great need for spiritual revival and the need to identify appropriate methods of evangelism occupied a prominent place and were constantly recurring themes. In 1942 the Association felt that its future could best be carried on by forming committees that would specialise in one area of work. The six committees that were formed were Youth, Women, Evangelism, Church Extension, Moral Welfare and Lay Preachers. Although war conditions limited what could be done, through time these committees made a valuable contribution to the life and work of the churches.

Shortly before the end of the war the churches in Westmorland suffered a great loss in the death of Mr A H Burra of Crosby Garrett. For forty one years he had served as secretary and treasurer of the Westmorland Group of Churches, and for most of these years he was active in the work of the Association. He was widely recognised as an expert in agricultural knowledge, and throughout the county of Westmorland he was highly respected as a County Councillor and a Justice of the Peace.

In 1945 the Baptist Union held its November Council Meeting in Newcastle to support and identify with the Association in celebrating its 250th anniversary. The Lord Mayor of Newcastle gave a reception to Council Members, and Northumberland County Council gave the Union the use of its Council Chambers for their meetings. Thirty seven of the Baptist Union Council members spoke at Sunday services in almost all the Association churches, and a rally was held in Newcastle City Hall addressed by the Rev E M Aubrey, Baptist Union secretary, and Mr Ernest Brown, MP, which was attended by two thousand people – certainly the biggest ever gathering of Baptists in the North East.

It is perhaps worth noting that it was at this meeting of the Council that the Baptist Union agreed a new financial structure that was to serve the Union and the Associations. Under this new Home Work Fund (later changed to Home Mission) all money previously given to the Association would be forwarded directly to the Union, and this funding would support all the work undertaken on behalf of the churches by the Union and the Associations. 25% of each Association's total giving to the Home Work Fund would be returned to the Associations for their own work, and a new Home Work Grants Committee would allocate grants to churches throughout the country.

For those who are keen on statistics, a comparison between the beginning and the end of the period covered in this chapter is of interest. It should be recognised, however, that it is not a comparison of like with like, since two of the churches (Thornaby and South Bank) with a combined membership of 375 in 1920 transferred to the Yorkshire Association in 1930, and so are not included in the later figures. The 1920 returns show a combined membership of 5417. Four churches had a membership of over 300, five churches had between 200 and 300 members, and a further thirteen churches had a membership of between 100 and 200. The returns also indicated a Sunday School enrolment of 7964 children and 1084 young people as members of either Christian Endeavour or Young People's Societies.

The 1945 figures give total membership as 4218. Stockton Tabernacle (which had 498 members in 1920) reported 501 members, the only church with a membership in excess of 300. Four churches had a membership between 200 and 300, and eleven had a membership in the 100-200 range. In 1920 there were nineteen churches with a membership less than 100, and that number had increased to twenty five by 1945, of which sixteen had less than 50 members. The 1945 figures also reveal a Sunday School enrolment of 4313 scholars and 636 young people attached to Young People's Societies. Although these twenty five years showed a decline in church membership of 16%, a more serious decline of 41% was seen in the number of children and young people attached to the churches.

# Chapter 14.

# Mixed Fortunes and New Challenges 1946-1970

The twenty five years following the second World War were times of mixed fortunes and saw the emergence of new issues that the churches needed to face. In addition to the formation of five new churches, six projects were begun with a view to establishing a Baptist witness in new areas, though sadly most of them for a variety of reasons did not take permanent root. The contraction in the coal mining industry and the closure of most of the collieries caused a migration from many of the pit villages which affected all the churches in these locations. New challenges had to be faced with the emergence of the charismatic movement and the growing movement for church unity. On both these issues there were strong differences of opinion, the latter causing some churches to withdraw from membership of the Association and the Baptist Union. In addition, the growth of 'the permissive society' throughout the 1960s with its resultant pluralistic outlook did not make any easier the spread of the Christian message in a society which was increasingly turning away from the churches.

**Expansion into New Areas**

Some Baptists who lived in Durham City began meeting together in 1949, and the following year they commenced holding regular Sunday worship services in the Shakespeare Hall in North Road. The work grew, and in 1951 the members constituted themselves as a Baptist church. At that time the Gilesgate housing estate in the east of the city was being developed, and the people began a Sunday School work there. Shortly afterwards the church moved there for their meeting place on Sundays and services were held in the St John Ambulance Brigade hut. In 1953 the church welcomed its first minister, Sister Freda Buckley, a Baptist Union deaconess. By 1957 the members began planning for the erection of their own premises. The local authority offered the church land in Edge Court, and their new building was opened in November 1959. Extensions to the premises were made in 1972 and further alterations were made in 1987. The church developed a good ministry to the students of Durham University, and by 1970 membership had reached about one hundred.

Also in 1949 plans for a new work in the growing housing estate of West View began to be considered by the Regent Street, Hartlepool church. A Sunday School was begun in January 1950 and soon had over two hundred children attending. In July of that year the church began holding services on the estate in the Civic Hut, and shortly afterwards purchased a site for a permanent building. A successful Youth Fellowship was commenced in 1951. As a result of several evangelistic events and missions the work grew, and many felt the time was right for it to be established as an independent church. In November 1955 the Regent Street church decided on this course of action, and in January 1956 at a special service twenty eight members were dismissed from the Regent Street church and became founder members of the West View Baptist Church. Their new building was opened in June 1957, and in 1969 an extension to the building was erected to help them in their growing work.

A post-war housing estate was also being developed in the Owton Manor area of West Hartlepool (the 'West' was dropped from the name in 1967), and in 1951 the Tower Street church secured an option on a site with a view to planting a new church there. In 1954, following a tent mission, a Sunday School was formed which initially attracted two hundred children, and they met in a local school. Later they moved to a new mission hall which they had erected in 1957 in Catcote Road, and began holding services in addition to their Sunday School work. This building was known as the 'Mackie Evans Memorial Hall'. The Rev Mackie Evans had been pastor of the Tower Street church from 1909 to 1947, and the funds for the erection of this building were provided by his daughter in memory of her father's thirty eight years pastorate. The building – a corrugated tin hut – was affectionately known on the estate as 'The Tin Hut'.

The local authority classified their building as a temporary structure, and imposed a time limit in which they wanted it removed and replaced by a more permanent building. In response, the members retained the interior, but changed the external appearance of the premises by building around and above the corrugated iron. In the first few years little growth was seen, but by the mid-1960s the work was beginning to prosper, and in May 1966 thirty eight members of the Tower Street church became founder members of the new Owton Manor Baptist Church. The work continued to grow and within a few years membership reached over one hundred. In later years to accommodate their growing work they erected building extensions in 1985.

Gateshead Borough Council was another local authority that undertook a large post-war housing development. One of the new estates was developed in the Beacon Lough area, to the south of the town centre, and in 1951 the Durham Road church began an outreach in that area. They held Sunday evening meetings in Derwent House Community Centre and also a Thursday evening women's meeting. In addition, they ran a Sunday School in the local school. The mission began to prosper, largely under the leadership of Mr Donny Rowe, and although those involved in this outreach desired to establish themselves as an independent church, some members of the Durham Road church wished it to continue as a mission outpost of their church. After some years, however, the Beacon Lough workers decided that independence would further their progress for the future, so in February 1963 in a service led by the Area Superintendent and attended by one hundred and twenty people, twenty three members of the Durham Road church became founder members of the Beacon Lough Baptist Church.

Attendances increased, an excellent youth work was established, and the need for their own premises became urgent. In 1965 a site was acquired from Gateshead Council for a new building, and this was granted on condition that the church erected a suitable building on it within three years. The church began encountering difficulties, not least in the raising of the necessary finance and pressure from the local authority, and they sought help from the Association. The Association appointed a management committee to work with the church and assist them in their developments. Eventually building work commenced in October 1967 with financial help from the Baptist Union, and their new building was opened in September 1968. It is worth noting that during this difficult period of the church's life their work prospered and fourteen people came to faith in Christ and were baptised in 1967.

In the 1950s Stockton Borough Council was developing the new Hardwick housing estate to the north of the town, and the members of Stockton Tabernacle accepted responsibility for establishing an evangelical witness there. With the help of Baptist Union loans and the giving of members a building was opened in November 1959. Although initially the plan was to regard the work at Hardwick as a mission outpost of the Tabernacle which would be run on much the same lines as the Portrack mission, it eventually became independent in 1968, with twenty nine members of the Tabernacle becoming founding members of the Hardwick Baptist Church.

In addition to the formation of those five new churches, two of the Association churches were relocated due to a compulsory purchase order by the local authority who wanted to redevelop their sites. Mention was made in the previous chapter of the three Baptist churches in South Shields uniting to form a new church in the Cleadon Park/Harton area of the town. Although they had purchased a site, plans for building had to be held over because of the war. In the years following the end of the war the project was revived, but a decision by the local authority altered the original plan. The church in Laygate Lane received notice in 1949 that it was to be the subject of a compulsory purchase order since the local authority were redeveloping the area in which the church was located. The three churches agreed that the new extension work would be replaced by the relocation of the Laygate Lane Church to new premises on a new site in the Harton area. The church's new building in Marsden Road was opened in November 1957, and was strategically located in the centre of a vast residential area. Within a few years as a result of vigorous evangelistic work in the community, the church saw its membership almost reach two hundred. Due to this growth the church built extra hall accommodation and this was opened in November 1971.

In 1956 the Enon church in Sunderland was also the subject of a compulsory purchase order, since the local authority were clearing the entire area with a view to building council flats. The last service of the church in their old building was in November 1958, and for the following five years they met in a local Methodist Church Hall until their new building was opened in 1963/64. Shortly after its opening the Rev Don Bridge became pastor and under his leadership the church undertook many new experiments in evangelism and within a short time their membership more than doubled.

A third church that was relocated in the post war years was Wallsend. Their new building was in the vast Battle Hill estate to the north of the town and was opened for use in October 1951. A new hall extension was erected in 1971. Since the church did not grow sufficiently to enable it to support its own full-time minister, it had either joint pastorates with other churches or was served by honorary pastors or moderators.

In addition to the building work seen in these new and relocated churches, several of the other Association churches undertook extensions to their existing premises. In 1949 the Blackhill church erected a hall on the ground adjoining their church building. The Billingham church extended its premises in 1955, and five years later built a new church hall. In 1970 the Oxford Road church in Hartlepool opened their new hall. Also, quite a number of churches had internal alterations and adaptations made to their premises to help them be more effective in their work and witness.

# The Challenge of the New Towns

One surprising fact of this period is that no Baptist witness was permanently established in the three new towns of Newton Aycliffe, Peterlee and Washington in County Durham, even though Baptists were fully involved in discussions about possible churches in all three locations.

In 1946 Durham County Council took advantage of the New Towns Act to build a new town adjoining Aycliffe village on the outskirts of Darlington which hopefully would provide employment for the unemployed miners of the South West Durham coalfield. The initial development of the town was quite slow, and it was not until 1981 that the town grew to its peak population of 45,000. In 1947 the Newton Aycliffe Development Corporation offered the Association a site for a Baptist Church and the Association agreed to take up the option. Two years later discussions took place about a possible joint work with the Church of England, but things were held in abeyance for a number of years because of the slow rate of house building. In 1964 the possibility of establishing a church was revived and following a conference of representatives from several denominations, the Association felt unable to have any further involvement mainly because of their inability to agree to a future financial commitment.

Three months after this, however, the three Darlington churches were asked to do some exploratory work about establishing a Baptist Church since a few Newton Aycliffe residents had moved into the town from areas where they had been members of Baptist churches, and they were meeting together on Monday evenings for fellowship. The leaders of the three churches met in July 1965, and since there is no record of either the outcome of that meeting or of any further meetings, it can only be assumed that it was decided not to pursue the matter.

The experience in the new town of Peterlee was a bit different. In 1949 the Association considered the possibility of a Baptist witness there and they put in a claim for an option on a site for a Baptist church. Since the site that was allocated was in an area which as yet had no housing, no action was taken immediately. The Church of England had set up a Bishop's Committee to explore the planting of churches in new towns, and since the Congregationalists had also put in a claim for a site in Peterlee, the possibility of a Union Church sponsored by the three denominations was discussed in 1958. The Association Committee had reservations about going in that direction. Apparently the Congregationalists had similar reservations and they withdrew their involvement. The Association felt the way ahead was the establishing of a Baptist Church, and as an initial step they canvassed the houses nearest their proposed site to get the reaction of the residents to having a Baptist Church in their community. Under the leadership of the Rev Reginald Panter, minister of the Marsden Road church in South Shields, twenty nine ministers and lay people from several of the Association churches took part in this visiting exercise and their report makes interesting reading.

They made 1224 visits, of which they got no reply at 370 houses, 43 said they were not interested, 421 said they were Church of England, 117 Roman Catholic, 118 Methodist, 12 Baptist (for most of them the connection was that they had attended a Baptist Sunday School when they were children), and 19 belonged to other denominations. 136 people expressed some interest in the suggestion that a new church be formed.

Following this survey, and the offer by Peterlee Corporation of the use of a room seating seventy people in the Eden Hill House Community Centre in October 1955, the Association began holding Sunday services and establishing a Sunday School work, which was largely led by members of Easington Colliery church. An Association Committee was formed, whose members included the deacons of Easington Colliery church to oversee the work. Unfortunately during the first year, attendances by residents were disappointing, with no congregation at all on some Sundays, and the Sunday School rarely had more than ten children present. In the autumn of 1956, teams of young people from the Association Youth Council visited the houses in the area, and in 1957 a tent campaign took place which was led by ministers in the Association. Despite these efforts, attendances at services remained small. The Association held a special meeting to discuss the situation since the Peterlee Corporation insisted on the immediate purchase of the site and a guarantee that a church building would be erected within three years. Since the Association was not in a position to accept this financial responsibility, they reluctantly decided to withdraw their option on the site and they discontinued the work, the final service being held in October 1958.

Washington was the largest of the new towns in the region, eventually reaching a population of 80,000 people. Whereas the other new towns were built on land that was largely underdeveloped, Washington was to encompass an area of twelve former pit villages. The new town was divided into 'districts', most of them retaining their original village name. Evidence shows that in such situations many people were reluctant to cross major link-roads to enter another district for any purpose, whether it was for shopping, entertainment or attending organisations. This indicated that establishing a town-wide church could encounter problems, yet establishing a church in each district was not a viable proposition.

In June 1966 the Association received a letter from the Durham Diocese of the Church of England asking if the Baptists were interested in a site for a church in Washington. The Association responded positively and over the next two years following correspondence and meetings, the suggestion was made that a united church be established. The Association referred the matter to the Enon Baptist Church in Sunderland since it was the nearest Baptist congregation and some of their members resided in Washington. Their minister, the Rev Don Bridge, agreed to attend meetings of the Anglican Bishop's Committee for New Towns to consider the future. Following several meetings over a period of eighteen months, a draft constitution for a united church was drawn up and submitted to the various denominations for their consideration and approval.

Although discussions were always cordial, everyone involved recognised that there were theological and ecclesiastical differences as well as widely varying financial structures within the various denominations. These factors weighed against the establishing of a "believers' church", and from then on Baptists had no active involvement in the discussions since the goal of the Bishop's Committee was the establishing of a united church.

Yet the Enon church did maintain a continuing interest in Washington since several of their church members were residents. The church developed strong links with a Brethren church in Chester-le-Street which also had a concern for Washington. On occasions the two churches had united prayer meetings and interchanged preachers. The Chester-le-Street church eventually did establish a new church in the Rickleton district of Washington, which became known as Rickleton Chapel, and in subsequent years several members of the Enon church identified with this new church.

**Women's and Young People's Work**

In the years following the end of the war, two very encouraging developments that deepened fellowship among the churches were in the work among women and young people. The Association Women's Committee established an annual weekend conference at Saltburn and this made a major contribution to fellowship among the women of the churches. Applications to attend frequently exceeded places available, and sometimes a system of 'rationing' had to be introduced, limiting the number who could attend from each church. In addition, women's rallies were regularly held in various churches throughout the Association, and these events were remarkably well attended. A Women's Rally was always a well supported event at the Association Annual Assembly. The women's work had a two-fold thrust – the Baptist Women's League (BWL) and the Women's Missionary Association (WMA). The purpose of the WMA was to encourage support for and interest in the work of the Baptist Missionary Society and usually their meetings were addressed by BMS missionaries or BMS home staff.

The Association Youth Council, which was formed in 1953, became increasingly active with an impressive annual programme of events which was well supported by young people from many churches. They held an annual weekend conference in Saltburn, and some years this was oversubscribed, resulting in applications to attend having to be turned down. The Youth Rally was an important part of the Annual Association Assembly, with attendances sometimes in excess of five hundred young people. Each year they also held a Missionary Youth Conference. For several years they organised two or three coaches to take young people to the Annual Scottish Baptist Youth Rally. They arranged two 'Youth Challenge Courses' each year to encourage young people to committed Christian discipleship. They also helped to establish inter-denominational Youth Councils in one or two areas so that they could work with the young people of other denominational churches in ministry to young people. Their magazine 'Outreach' was published three times each year and circulated to all the Association churches. In addition, they occasionally organised teams to lead evangelistic events and take services in some of our churches. Miss Rosemary Pollard, who had been one of the main driving forces behind the Association youth work, was appointed chairperson of the National Council of the Baptist Youth Movement. It was only in the early 1970s that support for the activities and events of the Youth Council began to lessen.

## The Charismatic and Ecumenical Movements

Two issues that were to cause divisions among and in the churches, and on which a common mind was never reached, were the rise of the charismatic movement and the movement for church unity. The Association's Annual Report for 1963 stated that some churches were beginning to feel the effect of the charismatic movement with its new styles of worship and emphasis on the gifts of the Spirit. Initially, its effect was seen in small numbers of people resigning their church membership and identifying with the emerging 'house churches'. As time passed, some members began to actively give their energies towards their own churches embracing the main features of the movement, believing that this was the way to the renewal of the church after fifty years of decline. Some churches resisted this move, believing that the movement was a challenge to Christian orthodoxy (one church even changed its constitution to prevent it making any inroads!). Through time, most of the churches recognised that the charismatic renewal had many valuable insights which could benefit the churches, but the extent to which these were adopted varied greatly from church to church. Probably one reason for hesitation on the part of some churches was that they had experienced some people who identified with the renewal movement who seemed more interested in novelty and sensation rather than authentic spiritual renewal. Although churches and individuals took varying attitudes, these were not regarded as serious enough to cause division or break fellowship.

Unfortunately the same cannot be said concerning the movement for church unity. The issue began to come to the attention of the Association in 1951 when Dr Ernest Payne, secretary of the Baptist Union, wrote to the Associations expressing the need for Baptists to come to a clearer view of their relationships with the other denominations. It was only, however, when the British Council of Churches held a major Faith and Order Conference in 1964 that the issue became acute. The final act of the conference was to call the churches to covenant together to work and pray for visible organic unity, daring to hope that the union of the churches would be realised no later than Easter 1980. Before considering the issue in detail the Association decided to await the response of the Baptist Union.

Early in 1967 the Baptist Union produced a report, 'Baptists and Unity' and sent a copy to all ministers and church secretaries. Although the report affirmed the rightness of Baptists remaining in the ecumenical process, it also affirmed that it would be a mistake for the Baptist Union to press for organic union by 1980. Despite the cautious nature of the report, there were many within the Association who identified with two national groups of conservative evangelicals who saw the ecumenical issue as a threat to a clear evangelical witness and felt that withdrawal from all involvement in it was the proper course to be followed. These two groups were the Baptist Revival Fellowship which was formed in the 1930s and gathered strength in the 1960s and 1970s, an the British Evangelical Council which was formed in 1953 and was greatly strengthened in the 1960s by the support of Dr Martyn Lloyd-Jones and the Westminster Fellowship of which he was leader. The views of those in the Association who supported one or both of these organisations largely determined the Association's response, and in 1967 it sent a resolution to the Baptist Union saying that many within the Northern

Association felt that the 'Baptists and Unity' report did not adequately reflect the true position in the denomination and that the Committee which produced the report would be improved by having some members who represent the anti-ecumenical position (it should be noted, however, that some of the committee members were of that position). The Association Annual report in 1967 stated that "the ferment in church relations is affecting us all and decisions about this in the near future could have far reaching repercussions".

By 1969 disquiet was being acknowledged and some in the Association were questioning their denominational loyalty. By the end of that year the emphasis on discussions in the Association had shifted from the contents of the 'Baptists and Unity' report, to whether or not the Baptist Union Council was really the voice of grass roots Baptists. As mentioned above, most ministers and churches in the Association were of a conservative theological outlook, and many of them felt the Council of the Union was disproportionately made up of people who were liberal in their theological views and who were committed to ecumenical action. To some this was unacceptable, and the fact that the Association did not give an outright rejection of the Baptist Union report resulted in the three churches at Lightfoot Grove (Stockton), Tower Street (Hartlepool) and Geneva Road (Darlington) withdrawing from membership of the Association and the Baptist Union, and their resignations were accepted with deep regret.

The matter of the Baptist Union Council being unrepresentative of most Baptists was to receive increased attention on a separate issue two years later, but it was another eight or nine years before many in the Association felt that this situation had been adequately addressed.

The important issue of inter-church relationships and church unity, however, could not go away, since all recognised that the unity of the church was an important element of Biblical teaching. The dominant view in the Association was that Biblical unity cannot be divorced from Biblical truth, and their cautious, even negative, attitude towards the trend in ecumenical relationships was based on the feeling that insufficient attention was being placed on what constituted fundamental Christian belief. But as the years went on, the pressure on working towards organic unity decreased, and the Association developed a more positive approach to inter-church relationships, entering into discussions with and being involved in joint action with other Christian denominations.

## Changes and Challenges

The closing of many of the Durham mines in the 1950s and 1960s affected all the churches in the South West Durham coalfield. In the first twenty five years after the war the eight churches that existed in these pit villages saw their combined membership decline from 364 to 218. Several of the churches linked together for pastoral oversight, but arrangements for this were never wholly satisfactory or long-lasting and did not halt the downward trend. When the secretary of the Witton Park church died in 1962 the four remaining members decided to close the church. Even the church at Bishop Auckland (the largest of the mining towns with a population of 25,000) experienced difficulty in maintaining their work, and in 1964 the members decided to close the church. On hearing this news, the Association asked the members to reconsider their decision, which they did, and the Association accepted responsibility for the church and arranged for ministers and lay preachers of other Association churches to conduct the Sunday services. Sadly the church continued to decline and in June 1972 with only six members, the church decided to discontinue holding services. However, under the leadership of the newly appointed Association Minister, the Rev Edgar Wright, services were restarted in December 1972 and significant growth took place in the following years.

In addition to the closure in 1962 of the Witton Park Church, four other Association churches closed during this period. In 1947 the Middleton-in-Teesdale church informed the Association that it was in a very low state of health, with some members living too far away to attend services. The Association met with the church to explore ways in which it could continue its witness, but nothing concrete resulted. The members decided to close the church and it held its final service in October 1948. A few of the remaining members linked up with the church in the nearby village of Egglesburn. This church was affiliated to the Association, and the Association gave help in its ongoing work, but in 1973 the church withdrew its membership of the Association.

When the Broomley church relocated to Stocksfield and erected their new chapel in 1905, the Stocksfield church continued the arrangement of having a joint pastorate with the church at Broomhaugh, near Riding Mill. Membership and attendances at Broomhaugh declined in the years following the 1939-45 war, and in 1959 the church sought the trustees' permission to let the Methodists use their building, and in 1966 the building was sold to the Methodists, who continue to use it to this day.

The second bombing of the Lindsay Road Church in Sunderland in 1943 caused extensive damage and seven years were to elapse before the building was opened again for worship. During these seven years the members met with the Enon church, and then later in hired accommodation. When they resumed meeting in their restored premises in Lindsay Road in 1950, membership had seen a considerable decline. After several years of continuing decline and the fact that they were in an area with several churches nearby (the most prominent being the large evangelical Bethesda Free Church), the members decided to close the church. Final services were held in October 1966, and most of the remaining members joined the Enon church.

Another church that saw significant decline during the war years was the Emmanuel Church in South Shields. It had been started in 1892 as a breakaway church from the Westoe Road church due to differing views on conditions of church membership, and the members erected their building in Imeary Street which adjoined Westoe Road. Experiencing difficulties in maintaining their work, the members decided to close the church in 1953 and most of them joined the church in Westoe Road.

**New Thinking within the Association**

Throughout most of the twentieth century the Association expressed commendable care and concern for the well-being of the smaller churches, but limitations in the areas of finance and personnel meant that they were restricted in what they could do. At the end of the war in 1945 there were seventeen churches with a membership of less than fifty, and by 1969 another eleven churches had come into this category. During that period several ministers were questioning whether the time had come to rethink the patterns of Baptist churchmanship which had for so long been taken for granted. Prominent among those ministers was the Rev Arthur Liston of the Heaton church. He was moderator of the Association in 1959 and in his moderator's address entitled 'The Way Ahead', he expressed the view that radical change was necessary if the smaller churches were to be given the help they needed. He felt that the Association and the Union should have some authority over the local church, but because he realised the radical nature of this step, Mr Liston said that if any change was introduced it should be brought in gradually. Here we cannot do justice to the content of all that Mr Liston said, but some indication of its impact can be gauged from the fact that it was printed and received widespread national coverage, and was seriously considered by other Associations and the Baptist Union.

The Northern Association appointed a group to consider the implications of Mr Liston's proposals, and after several monthly meetings its members produced a report. Copies were circulated to all the Association churches for discussion and comment, and it received a mixed reception. Although the report created much interest, it would appear there was no consensus on what action should be taken.

The Rev Samuel Boyd of the Westgate Road church revived the issue in his moderator's address to the 1969 Association Assembly. His address was a searching examination of current Baptist practice and policy. While acknowledging that local autonomy may have been adequate in a former age, he maintained that smaller churches would continue to close unless there was a more dynamic approach from the Association and the Union. One possibility he raised took the form of a question, "Could we have a minister without charge for the NBA to go to encourage smaller churches for periods of from three months to a year or two?" The Association immediately took up this challenge, and within twelve months they had taken active steps to appoint a full-time Association Minister who would be financed by the Association, and whose primary remit would be to minister to smaller pastorless churches. A grant from Baptist Home Mission enabled an appointment to be made, and the Rev Edgar Wright was inducted to this office in October 1971. One interesting outcome of this step was that other Baptist Associations throughout the country enquired about this new venture, and several of those Associations in subsequent years appointed their own Association Minister.

Despite all the calls for evangelistic endeavour and the many mission projects undertaken by the churches during the period covered in this chapter, a continuing decline in numbers was reported. Membership went from 4228 in 1944 to 3373 in 1969, and an even greater decline was seen in the numbers of children and young people connected with the churches. Although the majority of churches experienced decline in numbers, several churches experienced fruitful evangelism and saw their membership more than double, so the downward trend was not true in all situations. To try and arrest decline, several churches in the 1960s introduced varying patterns of All Age Christian Education on Sunday mornings, but by the 1970s almost all had discontinued the practice, acknowledging that it had made little difference. It was an era of much labour and little return. Yet, despite discouragements, many churches continued to have evangelism high on their agenda, and continued to look to God to prosper their work.

Chapter 15.

# Signs of Hope 1970-2000

## The Association Minister

The coming of the Rev Edgar Wright as Association Minister in October 1971 was a great blessing to the Association and many of its churches. Mr Wright had completed a fruitful nineteen year ministry at Frinton-on-Sea, prior to which he had been a tutor at Regent's Park College, Oxford. When he retired in 1977 the 'Northerner' magazine printed a lengthy tribute, describing him as a pastor, teacher, scholar, evangelist, administrator and man of God.

The purpose behind the appointment of an Association Minister was to help the smaller churches in the Association. At the time of Mr Wright's appointment there were seventeen smaller churches with no pastoral oversight and a combined membership of 375. Mr Wright's first sphere of service was the recently formed church at Beacon Lough, Gateshead and his ministry was so fruitful that after twelve months the church was able to call its first full-time minister.

Mr Wright was then asked to serve the former Auckland coalfield area, and the five churches there agreed to form themselves into the South West Durham Fellowship of Baptist Churches. The Baptist Union had recently sold 'The Haven', a home for unmarried mothers, and they used the proceeds of this sale to appoint a social worker. They agreed to this social worker being based in Bishop Auckland to work with Mr Wright, and in 1973 Miss Enid Bichard took up residence there and her quiet, devoted ministry in both church and community over the next five years was a major factor in the renewal taking place in the Bishop Auckland church. In addition, Mr Wright enlisted the help of several lay people from other Association churches, and the work of this team provided a ministry to all the churches in the group.

One of Mr Wright's first tasks was to re-open the Bishop Auckland church in December 1972, since it had discontinued holding services six months previously. During the next three years that church saw over twenty five baptisms and among those who identified with it were several members with good leadership ability. By 1975 some of the churches in the group felt they were now in the position to call their own minister. On Mr Wright's retirement in 1977 the churches ceased to function as a group, and that year the Rev Eric Laing became pastor of the three churches in Bishop Auckland, Crook and Ferryhill. Under his nine year ministry the churches at Bishop Auckland and Crook continued to prosper.

In addition to his work with the smaller churches, Mr Wright's influence was felt throughout the Association. He enriched the lives of many ministers, and in addition became a mentor to several young men who were eventually to become leaders in Christian work.

## Churches Facing Decline and Change

Unfortunately, around this time several churches had reached such a low state of membership that their members decided to close their churches despite some attempts by the Association to revive their work. The Consett church, which had been established in 1867 by the members of the Rowley church, discontinued holding services in December 1971, having had difficulty in maintaining their work for several years. Several of the remaining members identified with the Rowley Church. A similar experience was seen in the Jesmond church in Newcastle. In 1959 the church considered closure since their membership was small and very few of them lived in the district. The Association helped them to maintain services, and in 1968 the Heaton church undertook a measure of oversight. Despite this help being given, the church continued to decline and the members decided to close the church as from May 1970. The Association held several meetings over the next two years to explore reviving the church, but nothing permanent emerged from this and the building was sold in 1972.

Although the Spennymoor church had been encouraged in the early 1970s by the team leadership under Mr Wright, it did not see any influx of new members. In 1979 the church decided to close since almost all their members were elderly and the church could not find members willing to accept the positions of responsibility which were essential if the church were to continue to function.

Also around this time the declining numbers in the Hamsterley church caused concern, and the holding of regular Sunday services became difficult. The church did not close, but established the practice of holding a monthly service, and for almost twenty five years Mr Angus Pearson of the Rowley Church served as lay pastor and conducted these services.

Another two churches which ceased to function in the 1970s were Benwell and Wyclif in the west end of Newcastle. At that period of time both church buildings were in areas undergoing extensive redevelopment with much of the housing being demolished. The Benwell church discontinued having Sunday services in December 1967, but they continued holding a Sunday School on their premises until 1973 with the Westgate Road Church assuming oversight of this work. In 1975 the Westgate Road church entered into negotiations with Newcastle Corporation resulting in the Benwell building being used as a community centre, but after some years due to vandalism it ceased being used and was eventually demolished.

The Wyclif Church had a similar experience to that of Benwell. In 1979 the church agreed with the Westgate Road church to enter into a 'Deed of Amalgamation', and final services were held in the Wyclif premises in October 1979.

The closure of the Jesmond, Benwell and Wyclif Churches meant that by 1980 there were only two Baptist Churches in Newcastle. Some indication of the change of Baptist witness during the century may be gauged from the fact that in 1911 the Newcastle/Gateshead Churches had a combined membership of 1461 whereas in 1984 it was 400.

In the 1970s the Durham Road church in Gateshead faced major problems with the fabric of their building. Some members favoured selling the building and moving elsewhere, whereas others felt they should remain. Unfortunately the differences of opinion over the issue became so strong that many members left the church. Several of the members lived in the Whickham area and in 1978 formed themselves into the Whickham Christian Fellowship. They met in a local school and in its earliest days attendances ranged between forty and fifty adults. During the 1970s the membership of the Durham Road church went down from 245 to ninety seven, and the members who remained in the Durham Road building were unable to tackle adequately the fabric problems, and over twenty years were to elapse before they were in a position to undertake the work that needed to be done.

In the last few years of the century the four churches in the Westmorland Group experienced changes. For many years the only two Free Churches in the villages had been Methodists and Baptists and not only did they often engage in joint activities, but marriages took place between members of the two denominations. The growth nationally of Local Ecumenical Projects

# Number of churches in membership with the Northern Baptist Association during the Twentieth Century

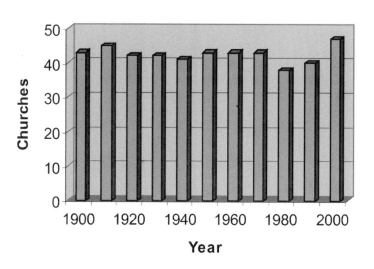

# Number of churches in membership with the Baptist Union during the Twentieth Century

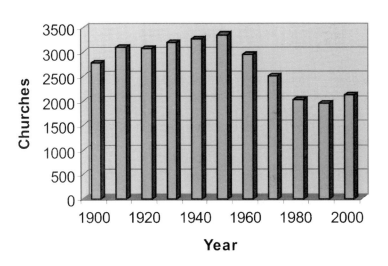

caused some of the members to ask if the time had come for this pattern to be adopted in this local situation. The Winton Church was the first to take this step and in 1989 they joined with the local Methodists to form the Winton United Church. In 1992 the Westmorland Group was formally disbanded leaving each church to function separately. The churches at Crosby Garrett and Kirkby Stephen were in a very weak position, and the Crosby Garrett church went in two different directions. Some members of the church for some time wanted to unite with the Methodists in the village, and in November 1992 they began meeting with them as Crosby Garrett United Church in the existing Methodist premises (the Sharing Agreement for this arrangement was not signed until 1997). The other church members, however, wished to maintain a distinctive Baptist witness, and in February 1993 the two churches at Kirkby Stephen and Crosby Garrett passed resolutions to amalgamate and form one combined membership which would meet in the Kirkby Stephen premises under the new name of Upper Eden Baptist Church. In the ten years following the amalgamation, the Upper Eden church more than doubled in membership, and continued to prosper under the leadership of Mr Roy Fellows.

Although it withdrew its membership from the Association in 1959, it is worth noting, though with sadness, the closing of the Tower Street church in Hartlepool. In its earlier years it was a church with a strong evangelical witness and had been active in church planting. In 1983 a division in the church resulted in several members leaving, and when many urgent and necessary fabric repairs faced the church, the remaining members found the cost too expensive for them to put the work in hand. Congregations dwindled and when by the late 1980s the numbers attending rarely reached double figures, the church closed in 1990.

**A New Emphasis on Mission**

Although it can be sad and depressing to record the closure of churches, the period covered in this chapter was by no means a time of decline and retrenchment. In the 1970s and 1980s the churches at Berwick, Stocksfield, Owton Manor (Hartlepool), West View ( Hartlepool), Stockton Tabernacle, Portrack (Stockton), Hardwick (Stockton) and Bishop Auckland saw their membership increase by well over 50%, and another nine churches saw a less yet nonetheless significant increase. In addition eleven new churches and congregations were established, and many of our churches made considerable adaptations or enlargement of their premises to help them to be more effective in their mission and service in their communities.

The following are brief details of some of the building work undertaken by churches. The Oxford Road church in Hartlepool erected additional accommodation in 1970. The Wallsend church opened their new hall in June 1971. In April 1972 the Durham church opened a new hall and three classrooms, and in 1987 made additional alterations to their premises. The Billingham church completed an extension in 1978. The Blackhill church opened their new hall in 1984. Owton Manor extended their premises in 1985. A tin hut which had served the Corporation Road, Darlington church for over eighty years was replaced by a new Church Centre which was opened in 1990. The Grange Road church in Darlington was faced with financial problems relating to the upkeep of their premises and held a church meeting in 1990 to consider selling their building and relocating elsewhere. After consideration the members decided to stay and develop their work from their present site. They adapted their premises, which included providing a Drop-in Centre for young people, and they became actively involved with other town centre churches in wide ranging community work. In the 1990s under the leadership of the Rev Roy Merrin, the Jarrow Church undertook a major modernisation of their entire premises which became widely used in a community action programme. The Beacon Lough church opened a major extension to their premises in 2000.

By the early 1970s an increasing emphasis was being placed on the need for more active involvement in evangelism. In addition to the work being done by individual churches, several joint ventures took place. The Rev Howard Baldwin, a Southern Baptist Convention pastor from Richmond, Virginia in the USA, visited the Billingham church in 1971, and as a result the Rev Robert McGrann, minister of the Billingham church, arranged a Partnership Mission led by Mr Baldwin in September 1972 which involved most of the churches in the southern part of the Association. Thirty three ministers and lay people from America led week-long missions in thirteen churches.

The positive results of those church-based missions resulted in Mr Baldwin being invited to return in 1975 to lead an Association-wide Partnership Mission. Under the banner 'Come Alive in 75', one hundred and eighteen American pastors and lay people led missions in twenty eight churches. Churches were encouraged to be ambitious in their thinking and planning, and many innovative methods of reaching out to the community proved fruitful. A key part of each church-based mission was an evangelistic meeting each evening. Most churches arranged for the American team members to visit local schools and speak at their assemblies. One head teacher was so impressed by the visitors that he arranged classes where the pupils could quiz them about life in the USA. Visits were also made to factories, colleges and Rotary Clubs. Almost every church arranged daytime evangelistic home meetings, and many also organised special events for children and young people. Almost all the churches reported conversions and re-dedications.

In 1982 the Association agreed to approach Mr Baldwin again about the possibility of another Partnership Mission and this took place in 1985. On this occasion twenty five churches participated and there were one hundred and forty six visitors from the USA. Reports from the churches spoke of one hundred and sixty first-time commitments to Christ in addition to many re-dedications.

When discussions took place in 1982 about this Partnership Mission, the reason for it being delayed till 1985 was that news was coming through of a Billy Graham Mission being held in the North East in 1984. 'Mission England' was to take place in five centres throughout the country, one of which was the football stadium in Roker Park, Sunderland where Dr Billy Graham would lead an eight-day mission from 26 May to 2 June. Evangelistic meetings were held each evening in the stadium, and during the day-time a wide variety of meetings addressed by members of the Billy Graham team were held throughout the region. Nearly every Baptist church was involved with 18% of the counsellors coming from Association churches and several Baptist ministers and lay people being deeply involved in the various committees. Total attendance over the eight days was 124,097, and 11,785 enquirers were counselled. Over 900 of these enquirers were referred to Baptist churches for follow-up, of whom 220 had no previous church connection. The USA Partnership Missions and the Roker Park Mission were contributory factors in the 10% growth in church membership seen in Baptist churches in the North East during the 1980s.

Another factor which contributed to this growth was the influence of the Church Growth Movement. The origins of this movement are found in the researches of Donald McGavran, a missionary in India in the mid-twentieth century. He observed that in some areas of that land the church was growing rapidly, and yet in other areas there was little, if any, growth. In his researches he sought to identify the factors that hindered growth and the factors that facilitated growth, and he published the results of his researches in 1955 in a book entitled, 'The Bridges of God'.

McGavran felt that people put different meanings on words like 'mission' and 'evangelism', so he coined a new phrase, 'church growth', and then defined what he meant by it. Here is his definition, "Church Growth means all that is involved in bringing men and women who do not have a personal relationship to Jesus Christ into fellowship with Him and into responsible church membership". This involves the church working for growth in four areas – maturity, fellowship, service and numbers – and in a later book, "Understanding Church Growth", he enunciated in greater detail factors that he felt should be present in church life if growth in these four areas were to be achieved.

McGavran's two books gained the attention of many Christian leaders throughout the world, and soon there began to emerge what came to be known as "Church Growth Principles". In the 1960s and 1970s significant growth was experienced in several countries where these principles were adopted as a basis of missionary strategy. Space forbids giving a full detail of all the principles, but three are worthy of mention here – the church's primary purpose is to make disciples not converts, evangelistic strategy should focus primarily on reaping a harvest and not simply sowing seed, and when people come to faith in Christ we should not expect them to cross unnecessary cultural barriers.

In 1978 a two-week consultation was held in London Bible College to see if the insights of the Church Growth Movement could be used with profit in the United Kingdom. The Baptist Union decided to send four delegates to this consultation, and I had the privilege of being one of these four. Following the consultation I circulated a document throughout the Association suggesting how these principles could be applied to our local churches, and following discussion of its contents it was agreed to hold a Day Conference on the subject. This took place in September 1979 and was attended by 225 ministers and church leaders – a remarkable turn-out for such an event. In the months and years that followed many of those who attended sought to implement in their own church some of the insights they had gained, and several churches reported that this had enabled them to develop a mission strategy appropriate for their particular situation. Although one hesitates to be too specific in linking cause and effect, it is not without significance that in the decade that followed this conference, membership of churches in the Association rose by 10%, the first time such an increase had been seen for sixty years.

As the twentieth century drew to a close, many acknowledged that while large mission meetings may have been appropriate in former years, their impact was decreasing. By 1997 many of the churches had begun running Alpha courses, a series of weekly meetings in a relaxed, non-threatening atmosphere where, by talks and discussion, people could explore the

135

Christian faith. This was to become one of the main features in their evangelistic work in subsequent years.

**Theological Differences**

As already mentioned, many people within the Association felt that the views of the Baptist Union Council were unrepresentative of grass roots Baptist thought, particularly in relation to ecumenical involvement. In 1971 another issue arose which seemed to confirm this view that the Baptist Union did not theologically represent the views of the churches of the Association. At the 1971 Baptist Union Assembly the Rev Michael Taylor, Principal of the Northern Baptist College, gave an address in which he seemed to deny the deity of Jesus Christ. One cannot do justice to Mr Taylor's address by quoting a brief extract, but the key issue may be discerned from these four sentences from what he said; "God indwells Jesus in the same way as he indwells his greatest saints and all of us. God is in Christ as God is in all men. Jesus is not of a different kind of stuff or substance. But Jesus is unique because God did something quite unique in Jesus."

At the meeting of the Baptist Union Council which followed the Assembly the Rev Stanley Voke urged the Council to repudiate the view expressed by Mr Taylor, but no action was taken. Within three months there was a groundswell of unease among Baptists throughout the country, not least in the Northern Association. The Association wrote to Mr Taylor about the issue and in his reply he said that he accepted the Baptist Union Declaration of Principle and did not regard anything he said as incompatible with it. The Association also wrote to Rev David Russell, Baptist Union Secretary, asking that the Baptist Union Council clarify its position. When the Council did issue a statement, rather than resolving the issue, it heightened the tension. Although the Council re-affirmed the doctrinal clauses of the Declaration of Principle, it added an addendum that "the Union has always contained within its fellowship those of different theological opinions and emphases, believing that its claim for tolerance involved tolerance and mutual respect within its own ranks". The Association again wrote to Mr Russell stating that in its view the Council had failed to deal unambiguously with the disquiet that was being felt.

Some indication of the feeling within the Association may be judged by the fact that some ministers and churches considered withdrawing from the Union. In addition, some of the ministers suggested that the Association resign its membership of the Baptist Union and apply for membership of the

Baptist Union of Scotland. When serious division seemed inevitable, this was averted by action taken by Dr George Beasley-Murray, Principal of Spurgeon's College. He wrote a paper, 'The Theological Controversy in the Baptist Union', and sent a copy to all accredited ministers. In addition he resigned as chairman of the Baptist Union Council so that he with Sir Cyril Black could present a resolution to the 1972 Baptist Assembly. This resolution declared that it was unacceptable to hold any interpretation of the Baptist Union Declaration of Principle which would "obscure or deny the fundamental tenet of the Christian faith that Jesus Christ is Lord and Saviour, truly God and truly man". The resolution was approved by 1800 votes with forty seven voting against and seventy two abstaining. Although this action satisfied the Association, one of the sad outcomes of this episode was that for several years the Association had no contact with the Northern Baptist College.

Despite this particular issue being resolved, the feeling that the evangelical voice was not adequately represented in Baptist Union affairs continued to disturb many within the Association. At this time a group of younger Baptist evangelical ministers, who affirmed loyalty to the Baptist Union, formed themselves into a loose grouping to address these issues, and their discussions eventually resulted in the creation of Mainstream. The purpose of this group was to provide a constructive influence in denominational affairs. Mainstream was publicly launched at a fringe meeting of the Baptist Union Assembly in 1979, which attracted an unexpectedly large attendance of 700 people. They then arranged a conference at Swanwick in January 1980 which received more bookings than available places. This conference was to become an annual event, and the movement went on to produce a regular newsletter as well as occasional publications. Many ministers and lay people in the Association churches identified with this movement, and through time most of the tensions that had caused unrest in the Association during the 1960s and 1970s largely disappeared.

Widely differing views about ecumenical involvement continued to make it extremely difficult for the Association to come to any consensus on what action to take. In 1977 the Association was invited to be party to a Sharing Agreement relating to a church that was being established in the new town of Killingworth. The attitude of the Association was that due to our Baptist ecclesiology it felt unable to make a decision on the matter, but would encourage individual Baptists who wished to be involved. A few Baptists did identify with the church and to express support of these members, the Association did eventually sign a Sharing Agreement, and in 1994 the Killingworth Church was welcomed into membership of the Association.

137

In the 1980s a new approach was made for Baptist involvement in the ecumenical church in Oxclose, Washington. The Anglican minister of that church, the Rev David Roberts, spoke to the members of the Association Committee in 1984 about the issue, and over the next two years several visits were made by Association representatives to the Oxclose Church. By 1986 it was evident that the Association could not make any commitment since the known Baptists who lived in Washington wished to continue operating as a home group of the Enon church in Sunderland. No further contact between the Association and the Oxclose Church was made after 1986, and this situation caused the Area Superintendent, Rev Tasker Lewis, to express regret at the lack of Baptist involvement in ecumenical affairs.

Another Local Ecumenical Project seeking Baptist involvement was the church in the developing Kingston Park estate in Newcastle. In its early days several Baptists identified with the church there which resulted in a Sharing Agreement being signed by the Association in 1995 and the church being welcomed into the Association the following year.

In 1988 the British Council of Churches arranged a major Inter-Church Conference in Swanwick, and its major conclusions were contained in the 'Swanwick Declaration'. This document was circulated to all the churches, and it was emphasised that all views about inter-church relationships should be freely expressed. Two new features that emerged from the conference were: firstly, an emphasis on churches working together in partnership rather than majoring on working towards organic union, and secondly, the inclusion of the Roman Catholic Church as a full participant. The first feature resulted in the British Council of Churches being replaced by the various Churches Together groupings. The second feature caused many evangelicals to have continuing misgivings about the whole Inter-Church Process. The Baptist Union at its 1989 Assembly voted in favour of being a full member of the proposed new ecumenical bodies, 1035 voting for and 364 against. Sadly this decision resulted in the church at Langley Park withdrawing its membership from the Association and the Union.

## The Association Minister and Missioner

Prior to retiring from the position of Association Minister in 1977, the Rev Edgar Wright submitted a paper to the Association Committee containing his observations on how a future Association Minister could best be used. The Association accepted his recommendations and agreed that this type of ministry should be continued and that a successor to Mr Wright should be sought on the basis of a new job description. Over the next few years several people were interviewed, but none of these resulted in an appointment being made. When Mr Abel Rees, a deacon of the Westgate Road Baptist Church in Newcastle, intimated in 1982 that he was resigning as Association Secretary, the Association decided to combine the positions of Association Minister and Secretary. At that time I was pastor of the Whitley Bay church, and was invited to serve in this office. I held this position from 1983 to 1988, and one of the major emphases during that period was helping smaller churches to a position where they could have permanent pastoral oversight. When Mr Wright was appointed there were seventeen smaller churches which had no pastoral oversight. By the time I concluded my period of service there were only two churches in that category, and it was evident that the position of Association Minister had largely served its purpose.

The Association felt that any future appointment should be that of Association Missioner, and that a major task of the person appointed would be the planting of new churches. The Rev Eric Westwood, who had recently concluded twenty years service with the Baptist Missionary Society in Brazil, began as Missioner in January 1989, and under an arrangement of joint funding agreed between the Northern and Yorkshire Associations, the area served by Eric Westwood included the Cleveland churches which at that time were members of the Yorkshire Association. Within twelve months of him taking up this work new congregations under his leadership had been established at Morpeth and at Coulby Newham in Middlesbrough.

Five families who lived in Morpeth and met regularly in one another's homes for Bible study and prayer had connections with the Heaton church in Newcastle. Eric Westwood met with this group and morning services were begun in a local Morpeth school in September 1989. Attendances exceeded everyone's expectations, and within five months the Morpeth Baptist Church was constituted with twenty eight founding members. At that time the church had an average congregation of seventy, and within a short time the church was seeking its own pastor. The church continued to grow and within a few years its membership more than doubled.

At the same time as meeting with people in Morpeth, Eric Westwood was meeting with a group in Coulby Newham who had links with the Cambridge Road church in Middlesbrough. This group was a follow-up to the church's involvement in the Billy Graham Mission '89 Livelink, a series of evangelistic meetings addressed by Dr Billy Graham in Earl's Court, London, and broadcast by satellite to venues throughout the country, including several in the North East. In September they began holding Sunday services with an average attendance of forty. During the next two years the congregation continued to grow in numbers, and in 1992 the Coulby Newham Baptist Church was established with thirty three members and they began meeting in the Langdon Square Community Centre. Over the next few years membership grew to over one hundred, and the church was able to appoint its own full-time pastor.

In 1992 Eric Westwood served as President of the Baptist Union, and the following year he initiated a major project by arranging seven regional consultations covering every church in the Association. Each church was asked to respond to seven preparatory questions covering their methods, difficulties and possibilities in evangelism. When he had received the churches' responses, he arranged a regional consultation to address the specific issues raised by these responses, with a view to identifying a practical strategy for evangelism which the churches could adopt. The replies from the churches give a revealing insight into how they faced the task of mission, many giving instances of evangelistic activities and events which they had undertaken. Although much commendable work was done, most churches admitted that this was undertaken by a minority of members, and that they experienced a low response rate in terms of people coming to faith in Christ. Eric Westwood spent the remaining two years of his time as Association Missioner helping the churches to implement some of the conclusions reached at the consultations.

**Renewal and Growth**

As mentioned earlier in this chapter, good things were happening in many of our churches, and what follows are brief portraits of some of these things. Space forbids going into much detail, but we hope there is enough information here to see how God's blessing was being known in many situations.

In 1973 the North Shields church reported that it was going through a very difficult time, with finances being inadequate to support their minister, and extensive dry rot being found in their premises. At that time I was pastor of the neighbouring Whitley Bay church, and the North Shields church invited me to serve as their moderator. With the consent of the Whitley Bay church I gave the church limited pastoral oversight for four years. In 1974 they put their building up for sale and considered meeting in rented accommodation because the church felt unable to meet the cost of fabric repairs which were essential to make the building safe. In June 1975, however, the church agreed not to sell their premises and decided to devote themselves to a programme of evangelism, part of which included participation in the 'Come Alive in 75' mission. On Easter Sunday 1976, eleven people were baptised who had recently come to faith and another baptismal service took place the following month. Further baptismal services were held in the two following years and the church now felt able to tackle the work that needed to be done on their premises, a considerable amount of the work being done by the members themselves. In September 1978 they were able to appoint the Rev Jim McGreehin as pastor. They demolished their old hall and built a new hall which was opened in 1979, and two years later they completed the renovation and decoration of their entire premises. By 1982 the financial situation of the church had so improved that they no longer required a Home Mission grant to support their minister.

In an earlier chapter mention was made of the Jarrow Church starting Sunday School work in the 1950s and later holding Sunday services in the Simonside area of the town. In 1978 a fire destroyed most of this building and its contents, and for a few years the congregation met in the lounge of a sheltered housing complex. In 1984 they took a lease on a building from the local authority which they completely refurbished, and in 1990 the members established themselves as Simonside Baptist Church.

In 1972 the Leng Memorial Hall of Stockton Tabernacle was the subject of a compulsory purchase order, and major alterations were made in their main building to compensate for the reduction in space caused by the order. In 1976 the church purchased the building adjoining their premises which formerly housed the Cooperative Restaurant, and this enabled the church to expand its ministry, including the establishing of a Christian bookshop. A significant feature at this time was a ministry by choirs under the leadership of Mrs Margaret Cornwell. The choirs presented special music at Easter, Christmas and during evangelistic missions, in addition to touring widely in the United Kingdom and the USA.

The ministry of the Rev Neville Atkinson at Stockton Tabernacle was one of the most significant ever seen in the North East. He became pastor in 1969 and during his ministry of twenty six years he established evangelism as a dominant feature of the church's life. He baptised 780 people who had come to faith in Christ, and this growth resulted in the Tabernacle becoming one of the largest churches in membership with the Baptist Union. In addition, an emphasis was also placed on overseas mission, and at one point the church was supporting eighteen workers who were serving Christ in other lands. Towards the end of the century, property developers were interested

141

in taking over the site occupied by the Tabernacle for a major retail development, and as a result the church was rehoused in 2001 in a magnificent new building in The Square on the waterfront of the River Tees.

In Whitley Bay the former United Reformed Church building in Park Avenue was put up for sale, and it was purchased by the Baptist Church in 1975. The church sold its premises in Oxford Street to a Pentecostal Church, and began meeting in Park Avenue, the service of dedication of the new premises taking place in September 1976. In 1981 the church decided to transform part of its large hall accommodation into a residential conference centre with bedroom accommodation for thirty two people. One of its primary purposes was to provide cheap residential accommodation to churches for youth weekends and children's holidays, and many churches and organisations in England and Scotland took advantage of this facility in subsequent years.

The Sunday School that was started by the Whitley Bay church on the Whitley Lodge estate in 1967 continued to prosper, and due to the interest of some parents a morning service was commenced there in 1992. A third congregation was begun on the Preston Grange estate in 1998, and by the end of the century these three congregations of the Whitley Bay Baptist Church were well established to meet the needs of the growing church.

The work in the Gilley Law estate in Sunderland which had been established by the Enon church in 1968 continued to prosper, and in 1984 a morning service was begun in addition to the evening service and the Sunday School. In 1986 it ceased to be a mission outpost of the Enon church by becoming an independent church. A large nearby housing development in the Doxford Park area of Sunderland caused the church in 1992 to experiment holding its morning service in Doxford Park while continuing its evening service in Gilley Law. After a few years, however, the members felt unable to sustain two meeting places and they reverted to holding all their meetings in the Gilley Law premises.

For seventy years Stockton Tabernacle had been responsible for maintaining the work of the Portrack mission, and in 1979 following the resignation of Mr Dick Sharp who had served as lay pastor for twenty six years, the church became independent. The Rev Roy Searle became its first full-time pastor in 1980 and under his leadership the church developed an evangelistic and social ministry which was looked upon by several churches as a good model for their own work. Membership doubled within three years and continued to increase in the years that followed. The local authority worked in partnership with the church in its work on the estate. In 1985 the church had two community workers with the Community Programme Scheme and by the following year there were five community workers and twelve care assistants based on the church premises. This increased activity resulted in the church expanding its premises. Through time many of those living in the estate saw the people of the church as a caring community to whom they could go for help, and this provided many openings for service and witness. Some time later in 1996 the church expanded its premises further by building a new and attractive sanctuary.

On leaving Portrack, Roy Searle for four years pastored the Enon church in Sunderland, and then in 1992 was seconded by the Baptist Union to work fulltime as one of the founder leaders of the Northumbria Community. From small beginnings the Community has grown in size and influence drawing from all backgrounds, ages and traditions. Drawing inspiration from the Desert and Celtic traditions the Community is exploring a new monastic spirituality. Companions and Friends of the Northumbria Community are now a global network of Christians bound by a common Rule of Life, Availability and Vulnerability. The Community's Motherhouse, the Nether Springs, is in Northumberland but other 'houses' and foundations linked to the Community's vocation and vision, ministry and mission are being established across Britain, Europe and beyond. Many from the Baptist family are part of the Community and three Baptist ministers, Roy Searle, Trevor Miller and Norman Cumming serve on the leadership team. The Community is very involved in issues of spirituality and mission, serving the renewal of the church and engaging with the emerging and fresh expressions of church networks. Roy Searle was elected as President of the Baptist Union in 2005.

In 1967 Mr George Breckon, an ex-farmer turned evangelist, planned to hold a mission in Northallerton and approached the Baptist Church for the use of their premises. The church readily agreed to this and offered their building in Valley Road free of charge. The mission proved fruitful and follow-up meetings were held for those who had come to faith in Jesus Christ. The church then invited Mr Breckon to be their pastor and he assumed this position in 1970. In 1973 his son Rodney and his wife Jeanette began heading up the youth work of the church and God blessed their work with a steady growth in numbers. In the 1980s the ministry of the church was shared by both father and son, but by the end of the 1980s, due to his father's advancing years, Rodney was taking the leading role. When congregations began to average one hundred and fifty, the Valley Road premises became inadequate to accommodate all who attended. In 1993 the church began

143

holding its services in larger premises, and over the next five years various venues were used. In 1997 the church offered to buy the vacant Lyric Cinema in High Street, and when their offer was accepted, extensive conversion work was done in the building, and on Easter 1998 the church held its opening services in their impressive new premises. The church has continued to prosper and has become one of the largest in the Association with a widening and fruitful ministry in that area of North Yorkshire.

For many years the Alnwick church had been one of the smaller Association churches in terms of membership, but in the early 1980s an increasing number began to attend their meetings. In 1985 new rooms were opened in the premises to facilitate their growing work. By 1990 the church was able for the first time for many years to have its own full-time pastor. The Rev Gordon Turner was inducted that year and during his pastorate of thirteen years the church grew to be a significant evangelical witness in Alnwick and the surrounding area.

In the 1960s and 1970s the church at Berwick almost doubled in its membership, and in August 1986 moved from their building in Castlegate to modern purpose built premises in Golden Square. Berwick was the most outlying church in the Association, being eighty miles from the city of Durham where many of the Association meetings took place. Since Edinburgh was only fifty seven miles away and the churches of the Scottish Borders Baptist Association were much nearer than that, the church discussed the advantages of identifying with the Baptist Union of Scotland. They decided to make the change and in 1994 they transferred their membership to the Scottish Union and were welcomed as a member church at its Annual Assembly that year.

During the 1980s the Westgate Road Church in Newcastle, under the ministry of the Rev Andrew Rollinson, saw significant renewal and growth through three key features: the 1984 Mission England meetings at Roker Park, Sunderland, the church's involvement in the 'Come Alive in 85' Partnership Mission, and a church renewal weekend in 1986 led by a team from Gold Hill Baptist Church in Buckinghamshire. In 1987 the church accepted involvement in a government-funded community programme and in 1990 a community worker was appointed by the church. With a renewed emphasis in evangelism the church at this time developed a significant ministry to students and for the first time in many years the church began to experience an increase in church membership. When Andrew Rollinson left in 1995, he was succeeded by the Rev Paul Merton, and under his leadership the church's ministry continued to expand. For several years around this time the church considered the need for the development of their premises, and eventually in 1997 extensive improvements and redecoration took place, making their premises an attractive and effective centre for mission.

The other Baptist church in Newcastle at Heaton at this time saw a real, if unusual, movement of God's Spirit. The Rev Jim Wilson became pastor in 1980 and during his fifteen year ministry the church regularly had congregations in excess of 500 people, and saw many conversions and baptisms. The large growth in numbers resulted in an increase in financial giving which enabled the church to have a ministerial staff of three persons in addition to appointing a church administrator. The church had twenty five house groups, and around 150 people met regularly at six am for their Monday morning prayer meeting. Not infrequently Sunday evening services lasted for four to five hours because of the evident working of God's Spirit among them. On several occasions Josh McDowell, the well-known Christian apologist, led six-hour seminars on the trustworthiness of the Bible with 650 people present. In addition Jim Wilson was approved as an associate lecturer by the Crusade for World Revival for the Christian counsellor training courses run by Selwyn Hughes, and the people who attended these courses at Heaton came from over thirty churches of various denominations in the North East.

Down through the years the members of Stockton Tabernacle have been the prime movers in the establishing of several new churches, and this found expression again in 1990 when they planted a new congregation in the Norton area of Stockton. In its early days an average of sixty five adults attended the services, and in 1994 it became independent of the Tabernacle and was constituted as Norton Baptist Church under the leadership of the Rev Graham Prest.

In 1986 a spontaneous desire among a few people for a Baptist witness in the Gosforth and Kenton area in the north of Newcastle resulted in Mr Guy Lawrence, a member of the Heaton Church, becoming the leader of a new congregation in that area. They met initially in a community centre, and in 1989 constituted themselves as Northside Baptist Church with thirteen baptised believers and ten adherents. Later that year they moved their place of meeting to a hall of the local Methodist Church, but within six months the Methodist Church became less welcoming in their attitude. The Kingston Park United Church invited the Northside members to join them and the members voted in favour, but certain obstacles arose which prevented this union taking place. Some Baptists were already members of the Kingston Park church, and in addition both the Heaton and Westgate Road churches had home groups in the district whose members wished to continue their links with these two churches. An uncertain situation arose which needed resolving and when Mr Lawrence moved from the district in 1993, the church decided to dissolve itself and the members linked up with other churches.

During the 1980s the churches in the Cleveland district which were in membership with the Yorkshire Baptist Association discussed among themselves a desire for greater links with the Northern Association due to the long distances they were having to travel for Yorkshire Association events, Leeds being about seventy miles away. By 1993 they had decided to transfer their membership to the Northern Association, and the seven churches were welcomed into its membership at the 1994 Association Annual Assembly. The Rev Derek Allan had become minister of the Redcar Church in 1985 and under his leadership the extension work at Marske was constituted as a church. A further extension work was begun in Ings in 1996 when a new congregation began meeting in a local school.

## Association Life

An experiment to foster fellowship among the churches was the arranging of an Association Family Day. The first one took place on the premises of the Johnson School in Durham in 1984. Over four hundred attended, and a programme of seminars, sports, workshops and worship made it an enjoyable day for all age groups. The event was repeated for several years, and many regarded it as one of the highlights of Association life. Another event which fostered fellowship among the churches was a united prayer event. In 1991 the Rev Eric Westwood arranged a Day of Prayer which was held simultaneously in eight churches throughout the Association and over three hundred were present.

For some years prior to 1958 the secretary of the Southern District of the Association was Mrs Winifred ('Winnie') Webb, a deacon and later secretary of the Grange Road church in Darlington. That year she resigned that position on being invited to work for the interests of the whole Association. She served as associate secretary and gave generously of her time in working for the well-being of the churches, becoming the confidante of several ministers. In 1974 she was elected moderator of the Association, the only lady to hold this office, since the position was abolished in 2002, and in recognition of her major contribution to its work, the Association made her a Life Member.

A deacon of the Westgate Road church in Newcastle who served the Association well was Mr George Clark. Among his many contributions were his services as Home Mission Commissioner from 1960 to 1991, and during that period he also represented the Association on the Baptist Union Council and served on several of the Baptist Union committees where he was recognised as an ardent advocate for the interests of North East England.

Another deacon of the Westgate Road church, Mr Abel Rees, gave sterling service to the Association over many years. He served as Association secretary for seven years and in 1984 was appointed moderator of the Association. During the following twenty years in which the work of the Association developed in several directions, he gave freely of his time, and his wisdom and experience proved invaluable.

During 1970s fellowship among the young people of the Association churches was becoming increasingly difficult due to lack of support. Miss Marjorie Wheatley served as secretary of the Youth Council for several years, but the inability to appoint a new secretary on her resignation in 1978 resulted in the disbanding of the Youth Council. Attempts were made to revive and re-structure it in 1986 and Mrs Jayne Scott of Jarrow offered to serve as Co-ordinator, but when Mrs Scott moved to Manchester in 1990 the Council once again ceased to function. A positive step to encourage youth work in our churches was made by the appointment in 1997 of Mr Matt Noble as Association Youth Specialist, who also worked part-time in the South Bank Church. In 1999 Mr Noble left to begin studies at Spurgeon's College, but in his two years of service the youth work in a number of churches benefited from his guidance and help, and this work was continued by Margaret Dimmock who succeeded him.

In 1966 concern was expressed within the Association about the growing abandonment in society of absolute standards of right and wrong, and the fact that new moral and social issues were arising to which the church needed to respond. A Christian Citizenship Committee, later renamed Social Action Group, was formed and its members arranged meetings to create awareness of issues and suggest guidelines for action by the Association and the churches. From the 1970s onwards workshops and seminars began to be held regularly and a list of some of the subjects covered reveals some of the many areas of concern on which churches were seeking help. These included unemployment, medical ethics, poverty and debt, depression, substance abuse, healing, ministry to the mentally ill and the Christian response to AIDS. Attendance at these events averaged about seventy, and several churches expressed appreciation for the help they had been. The

# Membership of churches affiliated to the Northern Baptist Association during the Twentieth Century

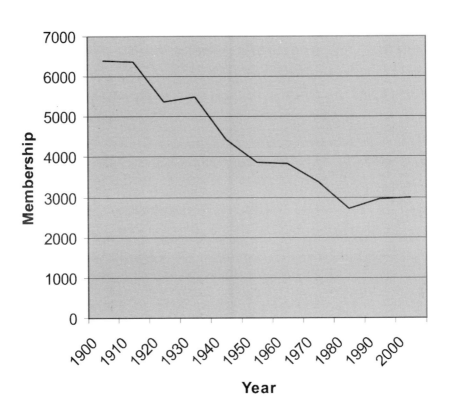

## Church membership of
## Baptist Union Churches
## during the Twentieth Century

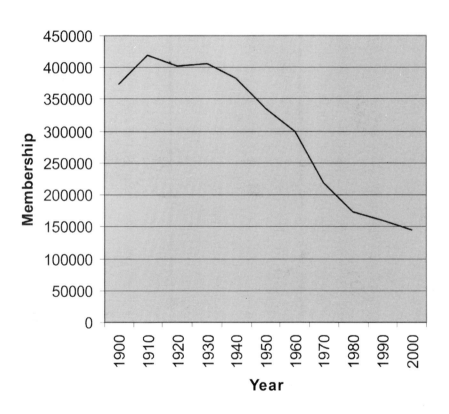

Association organised other seminars on subjects of a practical nature such as church administration, finance, and the information technology revolution and these also were welcomed by several churches.

When the Association was divided into two Districts, the ministers of each District met together regularly for fellowship. Shortly after the Districts were disbanded, it was agreed that one meeting would cover the whole Association, and due to its central location, meetings began to be held monthly in the Durham church. In addition, a residential conference for all Association ministers was held in Saltburn each year. During the 1970s and 1980s the monthly meetings were attended by nearly all the ministers and at these meetings discussions often took place regarding the future direction of Association and church life, and the decisions reached were fed into Association meetings, some of them eventually becoming Association policy. The Ministers' Fellowship continues to be a source of help and encouragement to those who attend.

One major step expressing Baptist involvement in society was the agreement by the Baptist Union to support a Baptist minister working full-time as an Industrial Chaplain within the Teesside Industrial Mission. The Rev Keith Argyle joined the T.I.M. team in 1974 and served in this position for nine years. The early 1980s saw great changes in the North East due to widespread decline in the mining and manufacturing industries, with some areas reporting over 40% male unemployment, and Mr Argyle regularly briefed the Association on relevant social and economic issues, giving suggested guidelines for action which the churches could take.

On Mr Argyle's departure to serve with the Salford Industrial Mission the Rev Bill Allen, minister of the Durham church, was appointed to succeed him in 1984 and he served for seven years until 1991 when he took up a lectureship at Spurgeon's College. The Baptist Union decided that the next appointment would be part-time, and in 1993 the Rev Graham Poole was appointed, dividing his time equally between industrial chaplaincy and the pastorate of the Thornaby church. Mr Poole concluded this joint ministry in 1998.

On the sudden death in 1995 of the Rev Brian Booth, pastor of the Oxford Road church in Hartlepool, the Rev Eric Westwood felt led to offer his services to the Oxford Road church, and on being invited by the members he resigned as Association Missioner. Although this pastorate was of only three years duration it was exceptionally fruitful.

When Eric Westwood resigned as Association Missioner in 1995, the Association spent many hours discussing what kind of future appointment should be made. For two years the committee explored the possibility of a part-time appointment to be shared with an Association church, but this possible arrangement was felt to hold potential problems, and it was decided not to proceed along these lines. Eventually a full-time appointment was made and the Rev David Hunt commenced as Association Missioner with special responsibility for mission in February 1999. Mr Hunt was widely accepted and soon involved himself in the work of several churches. However, due to the restructuring of the Association at the beginning of the new century, his appointment was only for a three year period, and his work came to an end before he had time for his ministry to become well established.

Shortly after taking up his duties as General Secretary of the Baptist Union in 1991, the Rev David Coffey initiated discussions about a possible improvement in Union and Association structures which would enable the work of mission to be more effective. Particular attention was given to the work of Area Superintendents, the nature of Association life, and the need to develop the Union as a resource centre for its member churches. Mr Coffey spoke at the Association's Annual Assembly in 1997 outlining how thinking was developing within the denomination, and by 1999 general agreement had been reached regarding the way ahead.

Two main changes came into effect in 2002. One was the creation of new Regional Associations throughout the country. Since 1915 the Northern Association had been linked with the Yorkshire Association by the Baptist Union for the purpose of Area Superintendency. Initially it looked as though this linking would be continued in the new structure with the two Associations being merged to form one of the Regional Associations. The Northern Association argued that it could be more resourced for mission if it were separated from Yorkshire and be regarded as a Regional Association in its own right, and the Baptist Union supported this position.

The second main change was the discontinuation of the Baptist Union appointing Area Superintendents. This was replaced by the Union giving financial grants to the new Regional Associations to enable them to appoint their own Regional Ministers. The Northern Association was thus able to appoint two Regional Ministers, one being responsible for pastoral matters and the other for mission.

151

# Chapter 16.

# Learning from our History

Inevitably when one explores church history, judgments are reached and comparisons made with current practice, and in this I have been no exception. So in this concluding chapter, without claiming any finality or originality, I dare to put in print some thoughts about issues raised by past history which in my view have a relevance for today.

## The Search for a Biblical Church

The main reason Baptist churches originally came into existence was a desire on the part of their founders to create churches that were a true reflection of the intention of Christ. There have been many attempts in church history at reform, renewal and restoration, and all have been based on the assumption that the only yard-stick that can be used to determine this is by a study of Scripture. The Bible is the source of our understanding of the true nature of the church's purposes, beliefs and structures. This was true of our Baptist forbears, and is seen in the fact that the earliest Association Assemblies were largely devoted to serious Bible study. The main thrust of these Bible studies was to enable the church representatives to come to a common understanding of the principles and practices that should operate in their local churches.

What were these church representatives looking for in their study of Scripture? The New Testament does not provide a uniform model for church life. The early churches in Jerusalem, Antioch and Corinth were not identical in their practice. Rather, Scripture provides the principles on which church life should be based. A model provides something static. Principles enable the church to adapt its life in the midst of historical and cultural changes without altering its message and purpose. I suspect that some, but not all, of the division and disunity that occasionally sadly took place in and between churches was caused by well-meaning individuals who insisted on a particular model of church life rather than focus on the Biblical principles on which their church life should be based.

Every generation needs to discover or re-discover the Biblical principles which should undergird church life, and this should be as important to us today as it was to the Baptist founding fathers. Do we judge all our church practices at the bar of Scriptures? If we are not primarily concerned about being a Biblical church, then there are really no grounds for maintaining a distinctive Baptist witness.

## What is a Local Church?

The independency of the local church has been a distinctive feature of Baptist churchmanship from the beginning, yet on at least four occasions within the Association some members felt that the issue of independency needed to be re-examined. These people questioned whether this was the best pattern for church government in all situations, especially those of smaller churches. It was suggested that smaller churches would sometimes be better operating on a circuit basis rather than each church struggling on in their independence. In practice this would mean these churches uniting with other churches in such a way that they would become one of several congregations of a larger 'local' church. After all, there was only one Jerusalem church, but probably dozens of Jerusalem congregations. This is not so 'unbaptist' as it may appear, because today some Baptist churches already operate in this way.

It would seem that the fundamental issue here is discerning the pattern of church government that would best enable each congregation to serve the interests of the Kingdom of God rather than regarding the independency of each congregation as something sacrosanct that must be upheld at all costs.

## Training Preachers and Leaders

The Esh Winning church is a fascinating study. For sixty-five years they did not seek a pastor from outwith their membership, believing that local lay leadership was the way they should go. During that period they were the only church in a mining village in County Durham whose membership exceeded 100. In fact, for a time they had nearly 200 members, which was remarkable for a community of 7000 inhabitants. Perhaps one key to understanding their vibrant life is found in the fact that a "Preachers' Training Class" was as much a part of the church's weekly programme as the Women's Meeting and the Christian Endeavour.

This training class no doubt not only encouraged the serious study of Scripture with a view to preaching, but created a body of spiritually mature people who knew their Bible well, and this in turn enabled leadership gifts to be recognised and developed. One outcome of this is seen in the active involvement of the Esh Winning church in planting congregations in new areas. In addition, on several occasions they offered their services to the Association when the Association embarked on some new venture.

How seriously do our churches today make provisions for the training of potential preachers and leaders from among their members?

## How successful are Joint Pastorates?

When churches entered into joint pastorates with other churches, almost always the reason was financial since the individual churches could not meet the expense of having a full-time pastor of their own. In the Northern Association very few joint pastorates saw much lasting fruit. Such evidence as there is indicates that this arrangement often caused tension between the churches, including such issues as the location of the minister's residence and the proportion of the minister's time being given to each church. These pastorates were rarely of more than four years duration, some lasting only eighteen months. On a few occasions some pastors were advised to leave to prevent a deteriorating situation getting even worse. Some joint pastorates, however, did see a measure of success, but the evidence would indicate that in the majority of cases there was little change in the church situations.

Although this seems a largely negative picture, we still need to address the issue of what is the most effective way to provide appropriate pastoral leadership of smaller churches. One problem is that many of these churches are primarily concerned about their very survival as a church, and this is understandable. A positive way forward would be to encourage the members of these churches to discard a survival mentality and instead focus their thinking on how they see their church in its relation to furthering the interests of the Kingdom of God. Making decisions about their future in that context could help them to come up with answers that would possibly more adequately meet their needs.

## Causes of Decline and Growth

There could be no end of comments on this issue! The earliest years of Baptist life in the North East saw very little growth. In 1800, which was 150 years after the founding of the first Baptist church in the region, church membership in Association churches totalled no more than 300. One likely explanation could be that during those years the main emphasis was on establishing the form and order of a truly Biblical church. This concentration on the church's inner life sometimes resulted in evangelism not being high on the churches' agenda.

The nineteenth century was one of significant growth. In the first half of the century church membership increased from 300 to 1287. Evangelism came to occupy a more prominent place, and the evidence would suggest it came about largely through the visionary leadership of a small number of pastors and evangelists who stimulated the churches to reach out to people and communities with the gospel.

The second half of the nineteenth century was the period of most rapid growth, with 1287 church members in 1850 increasing to 6386 members in 1900. These fifty years were also the period of most rapid growth in industrialisation in the North East, resulting in most towns greatly expanding in population and many new towns being established. Many within the Association and the churches felt that the aim should be to have a Baptist church in every community, and regularly the Association identified specific places that could be targeted. One main method used was the establishing of preaching stations, and although wholly accurate figures are difficult to come by, a rough estimate from the available information would indicate that during the century over sixty preaching stations were established in new areas, with over forty of them eventually developing into constituted churches. The main reason for some preaching stations not becoming permanent churches were the non-emergence of local leaders and a lack of response from the community. This would suggest that a major feature of church planting should be the identification of local leaders if a congregation is going to develop into a vibrant church.

In the towns of County Durham the main providers of activities outside the home were the public houses, Working Men's Clubs, Mechanics' Institutes and the churches. Public meetings, both religious and non-religious, were a popular features of that era, and many people would attend such events out of curiosity and interest. It was the response at such meetings arranged by Baptists that in most cases eventually led to the formation of a church.

The twentieth century in contrast to the nineteenth, was marked largely by decline. From a peak of 6458 church members in 1908, membership at the end of the century had gone down to less than 3000, and a far greater percentage decline was seen in the numbers of children and young people connected to the churches. No one explanation for this decline can be given, but the following observations may help in understanding the changing situation.

In 1911 the Association expressed the view that there was a change in the public mood and perception regarding church life, and recognised that the

155

interest and response shown by non-church people in the previous forty years was unlikely to continue. On several occasions both in Association moderators' addresses and committee meetings concern was expressed about churches having a maintenance mentality rather than being motivated for mission. It would seem, particularly during the period from the First World War until about 1970, that evangelism did not have a high priority on the agendas of many churches, some almost functioning as ghettos content with remaining in their existing position.

One reason given for the decline in work with children and young people was the lack of good leaders and of people with teaching skills. In the latter part of the century very few children whose parents were not church attenders continued their church contact after reaching the age of eleven years. In quite a number of churches the only children and young people attending were those whose parents were church members. Would the churches have been more fruitful had they concentrated less on children's activities and concentrated more on reaching parents?

Towards the end of the century several factors presented new challenges to the church in its mission. There was a marked decline in interest in religious and church institutionalism, yet ironically it was also a period marked by a growing interest in spirituality. The rise of pluralism and the rejection of absolute values caused many to view Christian commitment as merely a matter of personal taste and not a response to 'true truth'.

Yet despite all this, the twentieth century was not wholly a period of decline. Fifteen new churches were planted. In every decade of the century there were churches in the North East which experienced considerable conversion growth. In trying to understand the reasons for this I came to the conclusion that these churches engaged with their communities and that their evangelism involved face-to-face contact with people in their communities, rather than solely holding evangelistic events based on church buildings to which people were invited. Although there may be several sociological factors we can put forward to explain the decline in the twentieth century, I could not help but feel that one major factor was that some churches had a lack of confidence in the gospel and its power to change people's lives. Growth did normally occur in churches that seriously thought through and practised a strategy of mission that was culturally relevant.

## Church Planting

The desire to plant churches in new areas has almost always been present among the North East Baptists, though its success has varied from period to period. In the early years most church planting was due to the leadership of a few pastors who had a vision of preaching the gospel beyond their own local church, and were prepared to devote part of their time to fulfilling that vision.

The establishing of preaching stations which was so successful in the nineteenth century was largely initiated by neighbouring churches and their pastors who had a concern for a gospel witness in these nearby towns, and were willing to release some of their members to serve in these new locations. The main factor enabling these preaching stations to develop into autonomous churches was the emergence of local leadership. It was lack of this that prevented about one-third of them becoming permanent centres of Christian witness. This strongly suggests, as mentioned earlier, that a top priority in church planting must be the recognition and training of local leaders.

Some new churches came about as a result of Baptists moving into new areas for employment and beginning to meet together for fellowship. In many of these situations the Association provided valuable guidance and help which enabled these fellowships eventually to become established as Baptist churches. Almost all the churches planted in the twentieth century came into existence by this method.

## The Impact of Government Legislation

Since the Second World War, churches have faced increasing regulation both by national and local government, and this is likely to increase in future years. Although the ownership of buildings is not essential for Christian witness, it was local authority regulation that prevented Baptist church buildings being erected in new towns. For example, the local authorities of Newton Aycliffe and Peterlee generously gifted land to the Association on condition that an appropriate building was erected within three years. Having no financial resources for this kind of project, the Association had no alternative but to withdraw. This kind of experience was also known on some new housing estates. Has the time come to develop some kind of trans-local Baptist authority (preferably with financial resources!) that could respond to these situations, or do we continue to accept the consequence and limitations, as well as the advantages, of being independent churches?

157

Another factor that has come to more prominence since the 1970s is the desire to establish ecumenical churches in new areas. Is this the way forward for Baptist church planting? If not, it would seem that if we want to establish new centres of Baptist witness, the focus should be on using hired accommodation such as a school or community centre rather than seeking to erect our own premises, and making the church known through a high level of community involvement.

The growth of national government legislation affecting churches highlights the increasing value of the Baptist Union and the Associations in providing the necessary expertise to guide the churches in understanding and applying legal requirements to their local situation.

**Travelling to Church**

The last fifty years have seen the growth of car ownership, and it would now be safe to say that the majority of members of our congregations now travel to church by car. This raises a new issue concerning the mission of the church that was not present to the same degree in previous generations. A growing number of members reside some distance from the building in which they meet for worship. Although an extreme case, some years ago one of our Association churches had over forty members and only two of them resided in the town in which their church building is located.

Should the focal point for mission for these travelling members be the community in which they reside or the communities surrounding their church building? If it is the former, then an essential feature of mission would seem to be the establishing of a relevant home group where these people live, and which could be regarded as a base for mission to their immediate neighbour. Some churches are addressing this issue, but some still need to work out fully the implications of having a growing commuting membership.

**Having a Regional Vision**

Until the 1960s there were always within the churches of the Association a number of pastors and lay people whose concern for the North East caused them to demonstrate interest and give time and energy to the work of the churches beyond their own congregations. They had a regional vision. It was due to the growing lack of such people that eventually led to the appointment of an Association Minister in 1971. This was the first time the Association employed a paid member of staff, and this order of things developed even further when the Association was restructured at the end of the twentieth century. This development brought undoubted benefits, but one wonders if it has made our churches more parochial, and less Association-minded, since many now see the development of an Association vision and strategy as the responsibility of the paid staff rather than something demanding the personal involvement of people in the local church.

## Facing the Future

Many issues still challenge the churches as they face the future, and some readers may have wished that comment had been made in this chapter on other issues affecting church life. But perhaps enough has been said to stimulate thinking, so let me conclude with a few final comments.

Membership of Baptist churches in North East England is just over 0.1% of the population (nationally the figure is just under 0.3%). Around 90% of people living in the North East have no significant contact with any Christian church. A generation of children and young people are growing up almost totally ignorant of basic Biblical truth. These and many other facts highlight the need to develop a relevant mission strategy if we are to reach our present generation for Jesus Christ.

What should we do? Enlarging our church buildings is not the answer. Holding evangelistic meetings may have been appropriate for former generations, but these are largely, though not totally, ineffective today. It is becoming increasingly recognised that the place for fruitful evangelism is the community, not the church building. Acknowledging this, and in the light of our history I would suggest six essentials if we are to be the kind of churches that effectively serve our generation:

1. we need a confidence in the gospel and in its power to change people's lives.

2. we need a commitment to and a prominent place given to personal and corporate prayer.

3. we need an openness to the Holy Spirit to lead our churches in possible new ways. Why are we scared of being surprised by God?

4.  we need to be involved in service to the community as well as sharing the gospel message. John Stott stated this concisely when he said that for the gospel to be credible it must be visible as well as audible.

5.  we need to pray that God will raise up godly, visionary leaders who will challenge and inspire the people of God.

6.  we need an educated church membership that is able to speak naturally to non-church people about Christian faith and experience.

God has done great things in former generations. His power is no less available now than it was then. The challenge facing us is the same challenge that has faced every generation, namely, to play our part in becoming churches renewed for mission.

# Index